VERONICA MARS AND PHILOSOPHY

The Blackwell Philosophy and Pop Culture Series

Series Editor: William Irwin

A spoonful of sugar helps the medicine go down, and a healthy helping of popular culture clears the cobwebs from Kant. Philosophy has had a public relations problem for a few centuries now. This series aims to change that, showing that philosophy is relevant to your life—and not just for answering the big questions like "To be or not to be?" but for answering the little questions: "To watch or not to watch *South Park*?" Thinking deeply about TV, movies, and music doesn't make you a "complete idiot." In fact it might make you a philosopher, someone who believes the unexamined life is not worth living and the unexamined cartoon is not worth watching.

VERONICA MARS AND PHILOSOPHY

INVESTIGATING THE MYSTERIES OF LIFE (WHICH IS A BITCH UNTIL YOU DIE)

Edited by
George A. Dunn

WILEY Blackwell

This edition first published 2014
© 2014 John Wiley & Sons, Inc

Registered Office
John Wiley & Sons, Ltd, The Atrium, Southern Gate, Chichester, West Sussex, PO19 8SQ, UK

Editorial Offices
350 Main Street, Malden, MA 02148-5020, USA
9600 Garsington Road, Oxford, OX4 2DQ, UK
The Atrium, Southern Gate, Chichester, West Sussex, PO19 8SQ, UK

For details of our global editorial offices, for customer services, and for information about how to apply for permission to reuse the copyright material in this book please see our website at www.wiley.com/wiley-blackwell.

The right of George A. Dunn to be identified as the author of the editorial material in this work has been asserted in accordance with the UK Copyright, Designs and Patents Act 1988.

Wiley also publishes its books in a variety of electronic formats. Some content that appears in print may not be available in electronic books.

Designations used by companies to distinguish their products are often claimed as trademarks. All brand names and product names used in this book are trade names, service marks, trademarks or registered trademarks of their respective owners. The publisher is not associated with any product or vendor mentioned in this book.

Limit of Liability/Disclaimer of Warranty: While the publisher and author have used their best efforts in preparing this book, they make no representations or warranties with respect to the accuracy or completeness of the contents of this book and specifically disclaim any implied warranties of merchantability or fitness for a particular purpose. It is sold on the understanding that the publisher is not engaged in rendering professional services and neither the publisher nor the author shall be liable for damages arising herefrom. If professional advice or other expert assistance is required, the services of a competent professional should be sought.

Library of Congress Cataloging-in-Publication Data
Veronica Mars and philosophy: investigating the mysteries of life (which is a bitch until you die) / edited by George A. Dunn.
    p.   cm.
Includes index.
ISBN 978-1-118-84370-3 (pbk.)
1. Veronica Mars (Television program)   I. Dunn, George A., 1957– editor of compilation.
PN1992.77.V47V47 2014
791.45′72–dc23
                                              2014002207
A catalogue record for this book is available from the British Library.

Cover image: Girl holding camera © Cabriphoto / Getty Images; Lockers © P. Wei / istockphoto
Cover design by Simon Levy Associates

Set in 11/14pt Sabon by SPi Publisher Services, Pondicherry, India
Printed and bound in Malaysia by Vivar Printing Sdn Bhd

1   2014

This book is dedicated to A. B. "A long time ago …"

Contents
Mars Investigations' Philosophical Case Files

Acknowledgments

"I had my own reasons for doing it, trust me."

I am immensely grateful to all of the contributors to this volume, whose hard work is what ultimately made this book possible. You all delivered the Gold Package and I owe each and every one of your villages a goat. Another goat is on its way to the village of Bill Irwin, the general editor of the Pop Culture and Philosophy series, whose help and guidance were indispensible at every step of the way. This book could not have been produced without him.

In addition, Liam Cooper, Lindsay Bourgeois, Allison Kostka, and the rest of the team at Wiley Blackwell should be checking their lockers for fresh-baked snickerdoodles, as should James South, who offered valuable assistance at many stages of this project. Thanks for your hard work and support!

And, of course, this book would never have happened had it not been for Rob Thomas, Kristen Bell, and the 91,535 backers of the most successful Kickstarter campaign in history. Check your rooms, guys, for … a pony!

Introduction
The PI and the Philosophers

A long time ago there used to be a critically acclaimed television series with a devoted cult following. It was about a smart, savvy, and delightfully snarky girl named Veronica Mars, whose light blonde hair and pixie-ish good looks belied the hard interior of a jaded private investigator (PI) who was cynical beyond her years. Each week she would expose some new furrow of the seamy underbelly of crime and corruption lurking beneath the sunny façade of Neptune, California's mansions, beaches, and boardwalk. Viewers of the show learned to be perpetually distrustful of appearances, for nothing was ever what it seemed: a shy, geeky kid could turn out to be a psychopathic murderer and rapist; the adopted daughter of a local movie star might be outed as the secret love child of the current high school principal with the lunch lady; a successful restaurateur, baseball team owner, and glad-handing politician could be exposed as a child molester; and Deputy Leo D'Amato's police uniform might just be a tear-away. Anyone who simmers for very long in such a cauldron of deceit is likely to emerge rather hardboiled. But one might also, like Veronica Mars,

Veronica Mars and Philosophy: Investigating the Mysteries of Life (Which is a Bitch Until You Die), First Edition. Edited by George A. Dunn.
© 2014 John Wiley & Sons, Inc. Published 2014 by Wiley Blackwell.

emerge with a passion for the truth, and perhaps even for justice. Cheering her on, her fans formed a small but devoted band of "marshmallows," staking out our television sets week after week as she pursued these high-minded passions, as well as a few other passions of a steamier variety. And then, one day, Veronica cast her vote for Keith Mars for sheriff, exited her polling place, and disappeared down a Neptune street into a downpour of southern California rain and a deluge of scandal.

Veronica Mars was cancelled in 2007 at the end of its third season and, truth be told, some people hadn't thought of Veronica lately at all when, on March 13, 2013, Rob Thomas, the show's creator, and Kristen Bell, who starred as Veronica, announced that they were launching a Kickstarter campaign to raise funds to make a *Veronica Mars* movie that would bring us up to date on what happened to our spunky heroine after she disappeared into that storm. It soon became apparent that there are still legions of us "marshmallows" out there who care enough about Veronica to foot the bill for one more Mars investigation. To date, the *Veronica Mars* movie is one of the most successful Kickstarter projects of all time, with more than $5.7 million raised from over 90,000 backers—twice its official goal. As the first fan-financed movie adaption of a cancelled television series, not to mention its record-breaking number of Kickstarter backers, this is one for the history books. A little more than a week after Rob and Kristen announced the Kickstarter campaign, preparations for this book were already getting underway. *Veronica Mars and Philosophy*—what could be a more natural combination? They go together like Woody's Burgers and Little League. (Okay, that was an unfortunate comparison, so let's say Keith's homemade lasagna and watching *Slap Shot*.) After all, like our petite blonde detective, most philosophers are on fire for the truth, make ample use of the tools of logic, and recognize that things aren't always as they appear. We also engage in the occasional inner monologue, pondering the meaning of it all, and we have been known to misplace our copies of Søren Kierkegaard's *Either/Or*.

And indeed Veronica herself is a bit of a philosopher, though her philosophy tends to be a little on the *noir* side. *Noir* is a genre of fiction stamped by a pervasive mood of disillusionment, fatalism, and despair. *Noir* stories are typically set in a world rife with corruption and dirty secrets, where betrayal is the order of the day and the hero's cynicism is reinforced with each new seedy revelation. It's a world where, as Veronica puts it:

> The innocent suffer, the guilty go free, and truth and fiction are pretty much interchangeable. … There is neither a Santa Claus, nor an Easter Bunny, and there are no angels watching over us. Things just happen for no reason and nothing makes any sense. ("Not Pictured")

Veronica's bleak, pessimistic, *noir*-ish philosophy is summed up even more succinctly in her interpretation of Alexander Pope's famous philosophical poem *An Essay on Man*: "Life's a bitch until you die" ("Pilot"). But though her travails in the *noir* world may have left Veronica disillusioned, they haven't reduced her to wallowing in self-pity. Brokenhearted doesn't mean toothless, certainly not for this tough cookie. Her practical philosophy can also be summed up in a pithy maxim: "Get tough and get even" ("Like a Virgin"). Not every philosopher in this book necessarily agrees with all aspects of Veronica's code of conduct or with her assessment of the meaning (or non-meaning) of life, but we do explore key elements of the *noir* worldview in some of our chapters, as well as a busload of other topics.

If you're reading this book, chances are that you've already seen the *Veronica Mars* movie, which puts you at a bit of an advantage over the philosophers who have contributed to this volume, who, at the time this book goes to press, will have seen no more than the movie's trailer. The investigations in this book focus on characters and events from the television series and the philosophical issues they raise. And, just as there's no shortage of sensational crimes, tawdry misdemeanors, and lurid scandals to investigate in Neptune, so too our countless hours of surveillance in front of our television sets have turned up a treasure trove of philosophical questions tucked in alongside all the laughs, intrigue, and heat-stopping excitement. Though our methods of interrogation might seem a little tame compared to the ones Clarence Weidman claims to have learned at Harvard— no one was dangled by his or her ankles out a window in the making of this book—we think you'll still find some of our conclusions tantalizing, as we put our philosophical sleuthing skills to work investigating such issues as the racial and class divisions in Neptune society, the morality of law breaking, the nature of evil, and the injustices suffered by women at Neptune High and Hearst College. And, like good detectives, we ask some tough questions. Are Veronica's ardor to uncover the truth and her passion to see the bad guys punished always commendable? Is she a suitable model of what a friend should be? And can a gumshoe teach a philosopher about how to reason well? You don't need to be a professional PI to be thrilled at the philosophical mysteries we explore in this book. You don't even need a taser, just an inquisitive mind and a passion for *Veronica Mars*. So come along.

And be sure to take Backup.

Part I
VERONICA MARS IS RICH DUDE KRYPTONITE

INVESTIGATING POLITICS AND THE SOCIAL ORDER

Getting Past the Velvet Ropes

Status Anxiety in Neptune

William Irwin

If a visitor from a long time ago or from a culture far, far away dropped into Neptune, that visitor would be amazed by the great wealth not just of the Kanes, Echolls, and Casablancas, but also of the Navarros, Mars, and Fennels. They all have more than enough to eat, plenty of clothes, climate-controlled dwelling places with indoor plumbing, and cars and motorcycles to take them wherever they want to go. But it wouldn't take our visitor long to see that, despite the incredible base level of wealth, not everyone is considered the same. There are differences in status, in one's standing in society. Some are at the top, some are at the bottom, and, despite Veronica's description of Neptune as "a town without a middle class," some are in the middle.

These differences would likely seem silly to our visitor, who would consider all the Neptunians wildly wealthy. After just a little time in town, though, our visitor would be able to identify the problem plaguing Neptune: status anxiety. Everyone is worried about where he or she fits on the hierarchy of standing and importance. Our visitor wouldn't necessarily have to be human to grasp the importance of status. Some lower primates sort themselves, with alpha males beating their chests, feeding first, and

Veronica Mars and Philosophy: Investigating the Mysteries of Life (Which is a Bitch Until You Die), First Edition. Edited by George A. Dunn.
© 2014 John Wiley & Sons, Inc. Published 2014 by Wiley Blackwell.

claiming privileged mating rights. We humans would like to think we are above such vulgar displays, yet a quick glance at Neptune or at our own town reveals that we may be more subtle, but only a little.

Backup

Where we fit in, what our status is, matters. It matters to the way others treat us, but, maybe more importantly, it matters to the way we think of ourselves. And the two are linked. The way others treat us influences the way we think of ourselves. In his book *Status Anxiety*, Alain de Botton discusses both the causes of and the solutions to the problem.[1] Most impressive among the solutions are philosophy and art.

The phrase "be philosophical about it" virtually identifies philosophy with Stoicism, the philosophy that counsels us to determine our own feelings and state of mind without regard to what others think, believe, say, or do. Epictetus (55–135 CE), one of the leading Stoic philosophers, counseled:

> Remember that the insult does not come from the person who abuses you or hits you, but from your judgement that such people are insulting you. Therefore, whenever someone provokes you, be aware that it is your own opinion that provokes you. Try, therefore, in the first place, not to be carried away by your impressions, for if you can gain time and delay, you will more easily control yourself.[2]

Seeming to speak directly to Veronica on the eve of Shelly Pomeroy's party, Epictetus says:

> [I]f you have not been invited to someone's party that is because you have not paid them the price for which an invitation is sold. They sell it for praise; they sell it for flattery. Pay the price, then, for which it is sold, if you think this will be to your advantage.

But if at the same time you do not want to pay the one, yet wish to receive the other, you are insatiable and foolish. Do you have nothing, then, in place of the invitation? You have this—you have not had to praise the person you did not want to praise, and you have not had to bear the insolence of their doorkeepers.[3]

Epictetus believed that one's dignity and self-respect were far more important than one's status. That might seem an easy thing for him to say, though. After all, Epictetus had been a slave and had a crippled leg. He had no real chance of achieving status, and so it was easy for him to think that status doesn't matter. Yuck, those grapes you can't reach must be sour—right, Epictetus? Maybe not.

Another leading Stoic philosopher of antiquity was Marcus Aurelius (121–180 CE). You may have heard of him, especially if you saw *Gladiator*—he was portrayed in that one. Russell Crowe beat out Aaron Echolls for the title role. (I forget who played Marcus Aurelius—it was a small part.[4]) Marcus Aurelius was the emperor of Rome, the most powerful man in the world at the time. People like Jake Kane bowed before him. And yet he was a Stoic. After his death, the private journal of Marcus Aurelius was published as a work of Stoic philosophy, under the title *Meditations*. What did the most powerful man in the world have to worry about? Plenty. There were threats from barbarian tribes; but, more seriously, there were plots against him among his own people, including his own "friends." Even closer to home, his wife was having affairs. Marcus Aurelius could have gotten very upset and could have turned brutal and vindictive, but instead he turned philosophical, saying: "Will any man despise me? Let him see to it. But I will see to it that I may not be found doing or saying anything that deserves to be despised."[5] The Stoic emperor realized and accepted that the thoughts and actions of other people were beyond his direct control. At most he could influence them, and all attempts to have an influence would come at a price, often to be paid with his own serenity.

So two of the most important Stoics of the ancient world were a slave and an emperor. This gives us some hope that Stoicism could work in Neptune. But it leaves us wondering how it would work for someone like Keith Mars, who is neither a PCH-er nor an 09-er. Happiness is an inside job, that's the Stoic message. Virtue is its own reward, they would say. Through practice and effort you can develop your good character traits, your virtues, and no one can take those away from you, no matter what they say or do. Neptune society can kick Keith Mars out of office and label him a liar and a loser, but it can't take away his virtue and his dignity. He knows that he's honest, truth seeking, diligent, and intelligent. And he doggedly pursues the truth about Lilly Kane despite costs in status.

Keith is a mere mortal, though, and not exempt from feeling some status anxiety, especially on behalf of his daughter. Members of the Mars family have had to scale back their lifestyle, and Veronica has been ostracized by the 09-er crowd. Thankfully, like her father, Veronica has backup—no, not Backup the dog, but backup in the form of other things to make her feel good about herself. Sure she would like to have the approval and endorsement of the 09-er crowd. Who wouldn't? But Veronica finds that she can derive self-worth and happiness from many of the same virtues her father has: honesty, a dedication to the truth, diligence, and intelligence. And the approval of her father and of friends like Wallace and Mac is all she needs. As Botton says: "A mature solution to status anxiety may be said to begin with the recognition that status is available from, and awarded by a variety of different audiences … and that our choice among them may be free and willed."[6]

The Computer Geek and the Snitch

Let's face it, though, Veronica has one major advantage over her father. She's cute as a button, and not in some dumb-blonde way. Her sassy wit makes her otherwise dime-a-dozen Californian good looks something special. She's charismatic without being unctuous or ingratiating. She's confident without being arrogant. And this sure makes life easier for Veronica than it would be if she were the nerdy bookworm type. Speaking of which, her friend Cindy "Mac" Mackenzie doesn't have it easy and doesn't turn heads as she walks down the hall. Mac loves her family, but she doesn't quite fit in. They like NASCAR and camping, whereas she likes NPR and computers. It turns out that there's a reason for this: she was switched at birth with the despicable Madison Sinclair, who now resides with Mac's biological parents and exploits their wealth for all the status it will get her— including by throwing a lavish sixteenth birthday party for herself ("Silence of the Lamb"). Despite Epictetus' advice, Mac can't help but attend the party, bonding with her unwitting biological little sister and visiting the house afterward, to meet her biological mother, on the pretense of having left her purse in the library. Later, before leaving for a camping trip with her family – the Mackenzies – Mac sees her biological mother parked across the street. In a poignant scene, Mac walks up to the car. She and Mrs. Sinclair make knowing eye contact with each other as they each press hands against the car window.

Mac's life isn't bad. Still, she can't help but imagine how it would be better with her biological family. She seems to suffer from what Botton describes as "the feeling that we might, under different circumstances, be something other than what we are—a feeling inspired by exposure to the superior achievements of those whom we take to be our equals—that generates anxiety and resentment."[7] Mac would not, we hope, use the status of the Sinclair family the way Madison does, to develop popularity, but would avail herself instead of her parents' resources to develop her mind, as her biological sister Lauren has.

Who knows? Madison, too, may have been better off with her biological parents. Despite her life of privilege, Madison is not particularly happy; she wants to have more and more. Maybe, if she grew up with the Mackenzies, Madison would have been more appreciative of what she had and would not have become so acquisitive. Mac, unlike Madison, manages to make the most of her life. Although she doesn't really fit in with her family, she loves them; and, although she does not have Madison's 09-er zip code or Veronica's good looks, Mac still has status. She's smart and creative and unmatched as a computer whiz. Veronica befriends Mac and counts on her on numerous occasions to help solve mysteries.

Mac manages to feel good about herself because she has talent. Like most adolescents, she isn't brimming over with confidence and good cheer, but she at least avoids despair and feelings of worthlessness. Wallace Fennel, however, didn't seem to stand much of a chance at avoiding those depths. His career at Neptune High began with his being taped naked to the flag pole, as "snitch" was scrawled across his chest. Were it not for Veronica, there's no telling for how long he would have been hanging there. But an ostracized Veronica had become increasingly sensitive to the plight of the victimized and got him down.

As one of the very few African Americans in a school dominated by rich white kids and poor Hispanic kids, Wallace doesn't start with very good odds of establishing status. If he had some serious street cred, things might be different. But Wallace is not "straight out of Compton" cool. I mean, let's face it, he's not very cool at all. He may hang around with a pretty blonde, but they're truly just friends. How sad. As it turns out, Wallace has a source of status, though: he's a terrific basketball player. It's a little disappointing that the show perpetuates this stereotype. The black guy is the star basketball player and wins status that way? Come on. Rob Thomas could do better than that. The only other black male we see at Neptune High is Bryce Hamilton, son of Percy "Bone" Hamilton, the thuggish music producer who scorns his studious, bespectacled son for being a nerd who wants to get out of gym class. Of course, Bryce gets back at his father by ingeniously demanding ransom for his not actually kidnapped sister in the form of his father's beloved ring ("Lord of the Bling").

Bryce gains some status in his father's eyes as a result, and surely he has some status in the eyes of his teachers and the geek squad for his intelligence, but it's safe to assume that his high school life is otherwise rather unhappy.[8]

Lessons from the Navarros

Eli "Weevil" Navarro is way down at the bottom of Neptune's status totem pole. He's poor, Hispanic, without parents or good job prospects, and he's constantly in trouble with the law. Indeed he becomes a janitor, mopping the floors on which Veronica and Logan walk to class at Hearst College. Despite all this, though, Weevil is not without status. He is, at least for a time, a respected leader in the PCH Bike Club. He may not be book smart, but he's intelligent—Veronica's equal or better in navigating Neptune's underworld. Weevil is also tough. Despite being vertically challenged at 5′6″, he never hesitates to get up on his toes and into Logan Echolls's 5′11″ face. Indeed, Weevil fears no man. More than with any of the other characters we've considered, Weevil's status is self-made. Veronica, by contrast, was born pretty and was encouraged to do well in school. She can't take too much credit on those scores. Weevil has a grandmother who raises him and an uncle who looks out for him, but that was no guarantee for his gaining status in the PCH community. His toughness may be inborn to a certain extent, but, insofar as anyone can take credit for his or her status, Weevil can. This is not to say that he feels no pain.

Weevil envies and despises Logan Echolls and his ilk, people who have everything handed to them. He would have been glad to have been born on the other side of the tracks, with a silver spoon in his mouth and a pool in his backyard. To his credit, though, Weevil doesn't let his starting point in life keep him down. He makes his way in the world, even winning the affection of the lovely Lilly Kane for a time. Unfortunately their liaison must be kept secret, and so, while it fills him up inside, it wins him no status outside. The future may not be kind to Weevil, but there is at least hope. He has left the life of crime behind, and with his intelligence, toughness, and confidence he may well become a success—whatever that means.

And really what does it mean? It doesn't mean making a lot of money and getting hitched to a looker. Those things would confer status but they would not necessarily bring happiness. Just think of Aaron Echolls. And, although such things are within the grasp of Eli Navarro, they are not within the grasp of everyone. The average resident of Weevil's neighborhood does not have a good chance of attaining status. Weevil's grandmother, for example, worked for the Echolls cleaning their house, before she was fired on the suspicion that she had stolen credit cards from the family's mail. Of course the real thief was Weevil's cousin, Chardo Navarro ("Credit Where Credit's Due").

We do not get to know Weevil's grandmother very well, but we do see that she doesn't have any of the typical tickets to status. She's not particularly wealthy, beautiful, intelligent, or charismatic. Should we suppose, then, that she doesn't feel good about herself? After all, low status means low self-esteem, doesn't it? Of course not. Neptune is populated by plenty of high-status, low self-esteem people like Lynn Echolls. And there is no reason to think that Weevil's grandmother and people like her are without self-esteem – or even status – despite lacking the most noticeable status makers. Weevil's love for his grandmother—and especially his commitment to graduate from high school for her sake—tells us that she's a good person. She has dignity, and perhaps even status, which derive from her ability to do the right thing. As the Stoics believed, so Mrs. Navarro confirms: virtue is its own reward. She can be falsely accused and saddled with hardships, but she remains in control of her own virtue. Weevil's *abuela* (grandmother) has status in his eyes and, we can bet, in the eyes of the rest of her family and community.

Other People Suck

But the eyes of others are not easy to deal with, as the existentialist philosopher Jean-Paul Sartre (1905–1980) saw it. Veronica would probably agree with the bumper sticker "Mean people suck," but Sartre would take it further. Sartre didn't write bumper sticker slogans; but, if he had, one would be "Other people suck." Actually, Sartre said "Hell is other people," and that's more than worthy of a bumper sticker.[9] For Sartre, human relations are fraught with conflict. We are constantly labeling others in our minds, and those others are labeling us in turn. So we struggle to show others that we're more than, or other than, the labels they put on us, while nonetheless we continue to put labels on them. Veronica knows the feeling well. Lots of guys, including the captain of industry on the jury in "One Angry Veronica," look at her as if she's just a dumb blonde, and Principal Alan Moorehead and Sheriff Don Lamb look at her as if she were just a troublemaker. We, of course, know that she is so much more.

Digressing from *Veronica Mars* for a moment, let's consider the character Samad in Zadie Smith's novel *White Teeth*, who works as a waiter and has become tired of what Sartre calls "the look." Actually, on the basis of her experience as a hostess at Java the Hut, Veronica could surely relate. In comically poignant terms, Samad tells us that he wants to hang a sign around his neck that says:

I am not a waiter. I have been a student, a scientist, a soldier, my wife is called Alsana, we live in east London but we would like to move north. I am a Muslim but Allah has forsaken me or I have forsaken Allah, I'm not sure. I have a friend—Archie—and others. I am forty-nine but women still turn in the street. Sometimes.[10]

We can sympathize, of course. All of us have experienced being reduced to our momentary role by the look of the other, and we've all been guilty of looking at others that way—even Keith

Mars. The former sheriff's a pretty open-minded guy, but he disapproves of Veronica tutoring Weevil, because he sees the PCH-er as nothing but a criminal ("Hot Dogs").

It's all enough to make you think that maybe the best thing to do would be to drop out of society altogether. The great pessimistic philosopher Arthur Schopenhauer (1788–1860) said that "there is in this world only the choice between loneliness and vulgarity."[11] Indeed, he believed that "most society is so constituted that whoever exchanges it for loneliness makes a good bargain"[12] and that experiencing life in society makes one "as little inclined to frequent associations with others as schoolmasters to join the games of the boisterous and noisy crowds of children who surround them."[13] That may be a bit extreme, but when Veronica labeled Duncan Kane as a murderer through her suspicion, that was enough for him to take flight to Cuba, even though he was innocent ("A Trip to the Dentist"). The "look" of Veronica and the rest of Neptune was simply too much to bear.

Status Update

Philosophy may not cut it for you, at least not totally. Sartre's analysis of human relations and Schopenhauer's pessimism make it clear that being stoical is much easier said than done. So you may need the remedy of art. That's where *Veronica Mars* comes in handy again. Yes, Rob Thomas's *Veronica Mars* is art every bit as much as Da Vinci's *Mona Lisa*, Beethoven's Fifth Symphony, and Shakespeare's *Hamlet*. Okay, it's not as great as those masterpieces, but it's art nonetheless. And one of the important functions of art is therapy. Aristotle's (384–322 BCE) *Poetics* praised tragedies like *Oedipus Rex* and *Antigone* for their ability to produce catharsis – a kind of purging of negative emotions, particularly pity and fear. We don't have to experience the terrible fates of Oedipus or Antigone to identify with their misfortunes and dilemmas. Curiously, through our identification with these title characters we come away feeling not worse but better.

Aristotle also wrote a book on comedy, which unfortunately has been lost. Of course, *Veronica Mars* isn't exactly a comedy, but then again the kind of plays Aristotle was considering as comedies weren't exactly goofball sitcoms. Despite its *noir* sensibilities, *Veronica Mars* manages to be comedic, and sometimes even literally laugh-out-loud funny. We feel for some of the characters, but we can also see how silly it is to worry too much about what parties we're invited to and where we fit into the pecking order at the office. As Botton says: "Comedy reassures us that there are others in the world no less envious or socially fragile than ourselves."[14] It's in identifying with Veronica and other residents of Neptune that we can learn to laugh at ourselves.

Ultimately, when it comes to status anxiety, laughter may be the best medicine. So, for your next status update on Facebook, try this: "Watching *Veronica Mars* and laughing my way to feeling better." You'll get a lot of "likes," and that will make you feel better too.

Acknowledgment

Thanks to George Dunn and Megan Lloyd for helpful feedback on earlier versions of this chapter.

Notes

1. Alain de Botton, *Status Anxiety* (New York: Pantheon, 2004).
2. *Epictetus' Handbook and the Tablet of Cebes*, trans. Keith Seddon (London: Routledge, 2005), ch. 20.
3. Ibid., ch. 25 (translation modified).
4. I looked it up on IMDB (Internet Movie Data Base). It was Richard Harris.

5. Marcus Aurelius, *Meditations*, trans. A. S. L. Farquharson (New York: Everyman's Library, 1992), 82; compare Botton, *Status Anxiety*, 114.

6. Botton, *Status Anxiety*, 292.

7. Ibid., 26.

8. For more on race in Neptune and its intersection with issues of class, see Chapter 3 in this volume, by Regena Saulsberry.

9. Jean-Paul Sartre, *No Exit and Three Other Plays* (New York: Vintage International, 1989), 45. Strictly speaking, it is the character Garcin who says this, but the view fits pretty well with Sartre's view of interpersonal relationships.

10. Zadie Smith, *White Teeth: A Novel* (New York: Vintage International, 2001). Cf. Botton, *Status Anxiety*, 134. The text is printed in capital letters in the novel.

11. Arthur Schopenhauer, *Parerga and Paralipomena: Six Long Philosophical Essays*, trans. E. F. J. Payne (Oxford: Oxford University Press, 1974), 472; cf. Botton, *Status Anxiety*, 119.

12. Schopenhauer, *Parerga and Paralipomena*, 421; cf. Botton, *Status Anxiety*, 119.

13. Schopenhauer, *Parerga and Paralipomena*, 472; cf. Botton, *Status Anxiety*, 119.

14. Botton, *Status Anxiety*, 170.

"That's Really Criminal of You"
Why It *May* Be Okay for Veronica Mars to Break the Law

Paul Hammond

One of the things that we all love about Veronica Mars is her breezy disregard for authority. She's at her best when she's offering Sheriff Don Lamb a banana ("Silence of the Lamb") or putting on a fake accent to trick Principal Van Clemmons into giving her information about the bomb threats the school has received ("Weapons of Class Destruction"). Veronica generally scoffs at any of those who act like they know better than she does, and we usually think well of her for it—because we know that they really don't.

Sometimes Veronica's disregard for authority even crosses the line into full-blown criminality, and the show presents this as more or less of a piece with her character. Even in the "Pilot," we find her tampering with evidence in a criminal trial, when she arranges to switch the videotapes at the sheriff's department so that the two PCH-ers don't get convicted of shoplifting from the Sac N Pac. Of course, she does it with the best of intentions, but we have to admit that under normal circumstances something like that would be a serious offense. Breaking the law is usually something that we morally disapprove of, even if the offender

Veronica Mars and Philosophy: Investigating the Mysteries of Life (Which is a Bitch Until You Die), First Edition. Edited by George A. Dunn.
© 2014 John Wiley & Sons, Inc. Published 2014 by Wiley Blackwell.

seems to have good intentions. Let's say you were trying to smooth things over between your new friend and a motorcycle gang. Would you plant drug paraphernalia in another student's locker with the intention of starting a fire in the police evidence locker, so that your friend from the fire department could grab videotapes that were evidence in a criminal trial and switch them with ones that showed a sheriff's deputy soliciting a prostitute? Probably not. But what about Veronica?

Is there something unique about Veronica or about the place where she lives that makes it okay for her to do things that would normally be unacceptable? Or do we have to admit that, though Veronica's shenanigans are endearing and though we respect her for wanting to help her friends, she's still doing something morally wrong when she violates the law?

"I Failed Criminal Law and I Still Know that Can't be Good"

We would surely be concerned if any ordinary high school student decided to start taking the law into her own hands and engaging in illegal activities whenever it suited her, even if she did have noble intentions. But Veronica Mars is certainly no ordinary high school student. We learn in the very first episode that she has a unique personal history with the criminal justice system in her hometown of Neptune, California. In the year before the show began, Veronica, her friends, and her family were victims of some serious miscarriages of justice. Veronica's best friend Lilly Kane had been murdered and it appeared that Jake and Celeste Kane had covered up who really did it, which led to former Kane Software employee Abel Koontz's being wrongly imprisoned for Lilly's murder. Keith Mars, Veronica's father and the former sheriff of Neptune, had been railroaded out of office and publicly shamed for trying to uncover the truth about Lilly's murder. What's more, when Veronica later tried to report that she'd been drugged and raped at a party, the new sheriff, Don Lamb, not only refused to investigate the crime, but also treated her with an insensitivity that's shocking even coming from him.

Perhaps these miscarriages of justice justify Veronica's rather flippant disregard for the law. One could make an argument on her behalf that goes something like this. Normally I follow the law because it promises to protect and seek justice for me. In Veronica's case, however, the law didn't live up to its side of the deal: it failed to protect her and to get justice for either her or Lilly. Since the law didn't hold up its end of the bargain, Veronica doesn't need to hold up hers. Thus she's released from her normal obligation to obey the law.

This way of thinking makes use of an idea with a long and venerable history in political philosophy: the idea that, because of a kind of implicit contract or mutual promise, we shouldn't break the law. I get something from the law, such as protection and the assurance that justice will be carried out, and I give something in return by not doing the things that the law forbids. This idea has appealed to a lot of people who've thought about the organization of society, because it explains a specific moral obligation—the requirement to follow the law—in terms of a more basic one—the obligation to do what we've promised to do. We have to follow the law because we said we would. It's easy, of course, to understand why we would make that promise: we get something valuable out of the deal too. This contract isn't found in some document drawn up by attorneys. It's implicit— an unspoken but generally agreed upon arrangement. Though we never signed a piece of paper promising to obey the law, this idea of a "social contract" claims that we've agreed to the deal simply by accepting the benefits of living in a law-governed society. Accepting those benefits without paying society back with our obedience would be like walking out of the Sac N Pac with a couple of 40s in hand that we never paid for.

The notion of a contract also gives us a way of understanding how that obligation could be revoked in certain cases. When one party breaks a contract, the other party is released from his or her end of the bargain as well. Veronica clearly understands this way of thinking, as we can see when she encourages Carmen Ruiz to get back at her ex-boyfriend Tad Wilson after he breaks his word and releases an embarrassing tape of her to the whole school ("M.A.D.").[1] As Veronica sees it, Carmen is no longer bound to keep her word not to launch the website the two of them had designed to ruin Tad's reputation and sink his would-be naval career. Likewise, if the law is supposed to provide us with protection and justice in exchange for our obedience, but fails to hold up its end of the deal, then that might release us from the obligation to hold up ours. Do Veronica's past experiences with a justice system that failed to solve Lilly's murder and to pursue justice for Veronica make it okay for her to opt out of her end of the bargain as well? Veronica doesn't actually make this argument, of course, but we could imagine ourselves making it on her behalf in order to justify her unlawful behavior. But how clear-cut is this argument? Are there any objections that could be made against it? Let's turn to a philosopher who addressed a similar issue long ago and raised some points that might complicate our attempt to defend Veronica on these grounds.

"A Long Time Ago"

Plato (427–347 BCE), one of the earliest western philosophers, lived in the Greek city of Athens and wrote most of his philosophical works in the form of dialogues in which his mentor Socrates (469–399 BCE) is usually featured as one of the main characters.[2] In Plato's dialogue *Crito*, Socrates takes up the question of the citizen's moral obligation to obey the law. Socrates, in fact, finds himself in a situation that presents many similarities with Veronica's: he too has been wronged by the politically powerful in his city and is now in a position where he could plausibly argue that some good could come from his breaking the law. Socrates chooses not to break the law, however. Instead he presents a careful consideration of the moral issues surrounding legal authority and legal obligation, which is in many ways relevant to Veronica's situation.

Plato's account opens with Socrates in a prison cell, awaiting execution. A jury has found him guilty of impiety and "corrupting the youth of the city" and has sentenced him to death, though he's done nothing more than encourage young people to think for themselves and to question the city's political authorities.[3] Socrates' friend Crito, the character after whom the dialogue is named, has come to Socrates' prison cell and tells him that he believes the execution will happen within two or three days. Like Veronica, Socrates has gotten a raw deal from his city, but Crito tells him that he and Socrates' other friends are in a position to bribe the guards and sneak him out of prison so that he can go into exile and avoid execution. Though most of us would probably jump at the chance, Socrates won't accede to Crito's plan until Crito and he have considered the matter carefully from all angles in order to determine whether it would be morally right. They should ask themselves: "If we leave here without the city's permission, are we mistreating people whom we should least mistreat? And are we sticking to a just agreement or not?"[4] To answer these questions, Socrates says that they should consider what the laws themselves might say about the escape plan. He then reports the arguments that he thinks the laws would make if they could somehow come to life and be granted the power of speech.

Though it's not clear to what extent Socrates himself accepts the arguments that he puts forward on behalf of the laws, they do represent an interesting expression of the position that civil authority and the legal order might take in a case like this. How might society respond to the claim that past miscarriages of justice give a person the right to break the law in certain cases? The laws insist that, even though Socrates has been unjustly convicted and condemned to death, he still has no right to disobey the law, and they support this claim with several arguments that are clearly relevant to Veronica, if we think that her law breaking might be justified by her past mistreatment by Neptune's legal authorities. Let's consider these arguments and see how we might respond on Veronica's behalf. If the arguments of the laws are sound, Veronica is still wrong to break the law, even if injustice has been done to her and even if she's trying to promote justice by breaking the law.[5]

"I Get All My Criminal Tendencies from You"

"Do you think it possible for a city not to be destroyed if the verdicts of its courts have no force but are nullified and set at naught by private individuals?" the laws ask Socrates.[6] Here Socrates must consider whether any law breaking poses a potentially serious threat to the stability of society. The laws claim that illegal behavior leads to the destruction of the laws and of the city. However, there are two ways in which we might interpret what the laws mean by this statement, and Socrates' brief statement of the laws' position leaves both possibilities open.

On one interpretation, the notion of law itself contains within it the idea that a law must be universal or must apply to everyone in exactly the same way, without exception. Any law breaking amounts to an attempt to make an exception for oneself, destroying the law's nature and disrespecting the very notion of law, along with the whole social body. As the laws say, law breaking seems intended "to destroy us, the laws, and indeed the whole city."[7] To disobey the law would be wrong, then, because it would be tantamount to saying that the laws don't matter and it's everyone for him- or herself.

It seems clear that Veronica herself wouldn't want to say anything of the sort. Though she has little respect for the sheriff's department, she shows great compassion for other people and seems to want Neptune to be a place where everyone is treated equally by the law. But do her own law-breaking actions undercut this moral stance? There does seem to be a kind of hypocrisy in claiming to want a world where everyone is held to the same moral standards, but at the same time violating some of those standards whenever it suits one's purposes.

To defend herself against this criticism, Veronica could distinguish two levels of law: the actual civil laws of a community like Neptune and the more fundamental moral law. The German philosopher Immanuel Kant (1724–1804) made an argument similar to this, arguing that the notion of law implied its universality, and that therefore disobeying a law while expecting other people to follow it was always morally wrong. Kant, however, recognized that this argument applied only to the moral law, which might differ from, and even be in conflict with, the actual laws of some societies.[8] Using this distinction, we could defend Veronica by saying that, though she breaks the actual laws in Neptune, she does so in order to fulfill her higher and more important moral duties.[9] For example, Veronica steals Duncan Kane's medical file from his doctor's office to serve the higher moral imperative of exposing the truth about Lilly's murder and of bringing her real killer to justice ("Mars vs. Mars"). This defense might justify some of Veronica's law breaking, but probably only in cases where it was done for unimpeachable moral reasons.

We'll return to this idea, but first let's consider another way of looking at what the laws might have meant when they claimed that law breaking destroys the city. This second interpretation rests on the idea that disobedience of the law inevitably encourages more disobedience. Breaking the law is always wrong, on this view, because it encourages more people to break the law and drives us closer to the total breakdown of society. Criminality promotes more criminality. Even if your intentions are as good as Veronica's, you shouldn't break the law, because that only encourages more people to do so in less morally clear-cut circumstances.

This argument has something right about it. Any criminal activity could encourage the criminally inclined to be more brazen in their law breaking, and this is especially true of crimes that people see you get away with. The spreading disrespect for the law could eventually threaten the social order. When a murderer like Aaron Echolls walks out of jail a free man, we all feel less safe, not because we fear that Aaron will come after us next, but because of how his acquittal might embolden other potential murderers. Nevertheless, it's hard to see how this argument could prove that law breaking is morally wrong in every case. If the objection to law breaking is that it has bad consequences for society, then both the positive and the negative consequences of every breach of the law would need to be put into the scales and weighed against each other. Say Veronica has to steal some evidence from the sheriff's department in order to figure out who called in the tip that led to Abel Koontz's arrest for Lilly's murder. If this leads to Lilly's real killer being arrested, why can't Veronica argue that the increased respect for the law that results from bringing a felon to justice outweighs any decrease in respect that might result from Veronica's own misdemeanor?

Veronica might also call into question the idea, implicit in this argument, that the main thing holding society together is people's unconditional respect for the law and fear of being punished for breaking it. For a sleepy California beach community, Neptune has a lot of criminal activity, perpetrated by people who have far less respect for social order than Veronica herself. Yet civilization is far from breaking down completely. It's no utopia and certainly the local criminal elements, such as the Fitzpatricks, are destabilizing the social order to some extent, but Veronica could plausibly claim that the example of these criminals doesn't lead everyone to break the law whenever they feel like it. In fact, many of those who behave in pro-social ways that contribute to the maintenance of the social order in Neptune might do so more from an independent moral compass than out of respect for the civil law as such. We could make this same point about the real world. Threats of legal sanction discourage some illegal behavior, but exactly how much is up for debate. It's not at all obvious that people are civilized and well behaved primarily due to their distaste for doing things that are illegal. It might just be that the same behaviors that happen to be illegal are ones that most people would avoid for other reasons, no matter what the law said. If so, then a decline in respect for the law wouldn't necessarily lead to a breakdown in civilized behavior.

"That Community's a Lot More Wholesome and Functional than, Just for Example, Neptune Is"

The second argument that the laws offer Socrates concerns the idea of a social contract. We've already discussed how Veronica could appeal to the idea of a social contract in order to defend her law-breaking behavior: if the laws don't hold up their end of the bargain, then she shouldn't have to hold up hers. The second argument that the laws put forward addresses this move. There is indeed an agreement between the individual and the law; but, even if some individual, like Socrates or Veronica, suffers an injustice, that doesn't automatically mean that the laws haven't fulfilled their end of the deal. Specifically, even though Socrates was convicted of a crime and sentenced to death when he had done nothing wrong, the laws argue that they haven't violated their agreement with Socrates. Because his conviction took place according to the legal procedures that were in place in Athens, procedures under which he had agreed to live, he can't claim that it was the laws that wronged him. He was wronged by his accusers and the members of the jury that convicted him, not by the laws.

The laws can make this argument because they interpret Socrates' decision to live in Athens as a commitment to obey the laws no matter what, pointing out that, if he didn't like the laws, he had two options: he could have tried to change the laws through established means; or he could have left. His decision to live his entire life in Athens without ever raising an objection to its laws is tantamount to an endorsement of those laws. Does Veronica find herself in a similar position? She hasn't tried to leave Neptune, at least not until after her freshman year at Hearst College, nor has she fought especially hard to make its laws more just. Is she merely making an exception of herself?

Perhaps the first thing to note is that Neptune isn't exactly the Moon Calf Collective, which Keith describes as "a lot more wholesome and functional than, just for example, Neptune is" ("Drinking the Kool-Aid"). Those who voluntarily choose the life of communal dining and poinsettia-raising with Rain (aka Debbie Meyer), Django, and the rest can really be said to have endorsed that community and are free to leave at any time, as Casey Grant eventually does. But that's not true for every resident of Neptune, especially not for those who aren't millionaires like the Kanes and thus can't just transplant themselves to a new location whenever they're unhappy with the way things are going in town. Most people simply don't have the option of uprooting themselves and their families every time the laws displease them.

There's much in Neptune to be displeased about, of course. The sheriff's department, headed by Don Lamb, is at once surprisingly inept and remarkably corrupt. In "Credit Where Credit's Due," for example, Lamb and his deputy break up a high school beach party just to steal the keg. And consider the sheriff's department's inability to do anything timely to help Wallace Fennel and his mother Alicia get rid of the tenant who threatens them and refuses to pay his rent. As Keith tells Alicia, "I know how the law works. Slowly" ("Like a Virgin").[10] We could add many more examples of the ineptitude and corruption of the Neptune sheriff's department, but that would only belabor the obvious. Almost every episode of the show provides new confirmation that not only the sheriff's department but the town as a whole is corrupt. With an unfair social system that favors the rich and powerful over everyone else, Neptune is a place where obeying the law isn't always the best way to promote justice. Veronica's flashbacks to a time before Lilly's death show her living a happy life in a place that made sense and where she felt like she fit in. Outside the flashbacks, on the other hand, Neptune is a much darker place, where those in positions of official authority can only sometimes be trusted to ensure that the residents are kept safe and that justice is served.

Moreover, there are pervasive racial and economic injustices in this "town without a middle class." The sheriff's office seems to suspect Weevil and the PCH-ers of every crime that takes place, but special deference is shown to rich families like the Kanes. When the car Duncan is driving is pulled over and Deputy Jerry Sacks threatens to impound it for unpaid traffic tickets and an old moving violation, all it takes is the intervention of Jake Kane to get the tow truck sent on its way ("Credit Where Credit's Due"). Has Neptune revealed itself to be a place that's so unjust that its laws don't really deserve anyone's respect?

To couch this idea in terms of the social contract, Veronica could argue that the laws have failed to uphold their end of the bargain not just because of what happened to her or Lilly specifically, but because they fail to protect the citizens more generally and to ensure that justice is served for everyone. Socrates may be persuaded by the argument of the laws that, even if an injustice happened in his particular case, the laws on the whole have upheld their end of the bargain. But perhaps the laws have failed so completely to ensure protection and justice for all the citizens of Neptune that Veronica could say that they that haven't fulfilled the contract. The residents of Neptune—or at least the poorer residents, the ones who "work for millionaires," as opposed to their wealthy employers—can't count on the law to defend them and sometimes have to resort to other ways of protecting themselves, which perhaps explains why a relatively small town has such a booming private eye industry.

This isn't to suggest, of course, that the corruption in Neptune would make it morally permissible for Veronica to do anything she likes, criminal or not, under any circumstances. If Veronica claims that her law breaking is justified because social injustice invalidates the social contract, this argument would only allow her to break the law to encourage justice, not simply to enrich herself at the expense of other Neptune residents.[11] The Fitzpatricks, for instance, can't justify their own corrupt criminal enterprises by pointing to corruption elsewhere in Neptune. The failure of the laws to ensure a just society doesn't license the Fitzpatricks—or anyone else for that matter—to do things that are in themselves wrong. But Veronica can argue that she has no obligation to obey the laws when breaking them will do more to promote what's just and right.

This argument may make the setting of the show seem even darker and seedier than it initially appears, but it also casts Veronica's criminal behavior in a different and perhaps nobler light. Rather than just a saucy and snarky disregard for authority, Veronica's law breaking can be seen as a protest or civil disobedience, a refusal to accept the rules imposed on her by an unjust society. Sometimes when Veronica flouts the law, it may be more than just "really criminal" of her. It may also, on occasion, be really just.

Notes

1. For more on how Veronica comes to the assistance of Carmen, see Chapter 11, by Kasey Butcher and Megan M. Peters, and Chapter 12, by Jordan Pascoe, in this volume.

2. There has been much debate among historians and philosophers about how much the words that Plato places in Socrates' mouth in his various dialogues correspond to things that the real Socrates actually said or believed. The general points of Socrates' biography are broadly agreed on, but, since he himself didn't write any books or other philosophical works, we have no way of knowing

what he believed in any degree of detail. Since we're focusing just on one of Plato's dialogues in this chapter, however, when I refer to Socrates' views or arguments, I'll mean the character of Socrates as he appears in that one text.

3. Though Socrates was innocent, his snark-laden monologue at his own trial may not have helped his case much. Fans of cheeky, Veronica Mars-style disdain for authority can read Plato's account of this speech in the dialogue *Apology of Socrates*. Despite the title, Socrates doesn't come across as apologetic. The word "apology" in the title of the dialogue is simply a transliteration of the Greek word ἀπολογία, which means a defense speech.

4. Plato, *Crito*, 50a; in G. M. A. Grube, ed. and trans., *The Trial and Death of Socrates* (3rd edn., Indianapolis, IN: Hackett, 2000), 50.

5. The laws present several arguments, but we'll just consider two of them.

6. Ibid., 50b.

7. Ibid.

8. Socrates seems to have shared this view, even though he doesn't make this argument in the *Crito*. In the *Apology*, however, he reminds the jury of past instances when he disobeyed the orders of the legal authorities because they conflicted with his moral duty.

9. To be clear, though, Kant would probably not excuse her in this way, especially when it comes to theft and lying.

10. This episode is the occasion for the choice Keith Mars line quoted here, which illustrates the dubiousness of Neptune's legal system.

11. In light of this, it might be interesting to consider whether all of Veronica's deviations from the law are actually justified, or only some are. As an interesting case, we might wonder about her plan to charge her classmates "fifty bucks a pop" for dirt on their parents ("Silence of the Lamb"). Quite apart from considerations of legality, is it morally permissible for Veronica to do this?

3

"Got Any Enemies You Know About?" ... "Well, There's the Klan"
Race, Rancor, and Riches in Neptune, California

Rejena Saulsberry

I have a confession to make. When *Veronica Mars* first aired on network television, I dismissed it as *Nancy Drew* circa 2004. I wasn't interested in yet another drama about a girl with whom a twenty-something African American law student like me would never identify. Sure, there was a black guy in the cast, but he was obviously the obligatory minority best friend. I was much too cynical to expect compelling drama on that score.

After being badgered into giving the show a chance—and by my similarly cynical African American grad student sister, no less—I was happy to realize how wrong my assumptions about the show had been, particularly on the subject of race. Is it a perfect portrayal of racial diversity, with accurate and nuanced depictions of the modern American racial landscape? Hardly. My cynical side is doubtful that such a thing will ever exist. However, *Veronica Mars* offers something typically lacking in mainstream television. It confronts race, whereas similar shows have actively avoided the topic. The constant friction between

Veronica Mars and Philosophy: Investigating the Mysteries of Life (Which is a Bitch Until You Die), First Edition. Edited by George A. Dunn.
© 2014 John Wiley & Sons, Inc. Published 2014 by Wiley Blackwell.

classes and racial groups provides both the compelling drama that I'd hoped for and a narrative that was very familiar to me as an African American with her own experiences of class and race in this country.

"The Hero Is the One Who Stays and the Villain Is the One Who Splits"

When Veronica compares heroes to villains, she uses their oppositional nature as a way to define them: the hero does what the villain doesn't do, and vice versa ("Meet John Smith"). Ferdinand de Saussure (1857–1913), one of the founders of modern linguistics—and also of semiotics, the philosophical–linguistic study of signs and symbols—was one of the first thinkers to point out that we routinely use opposing characteristics such as these to define words or concepts.[1] While Saussure's work is typically of service in the study of linguistics, his ideas have also been used to explain how we interpret and define the world around us. His most revelatory observation is one of his simplest: we organize our world into pairings.

Consider Veronica's description of the student body at her high school: "If you go here your parents are either millionaires or they work for millionaires. Neptune, California, a town without a middle class" ("Pilot"). Veronica's description of Neptune's economic class structure introduces us to the binary or dual nature of its society. The traditional three economic classes—upper, middle, and lower—have been replaced by the "haves" and "have-nots." Upper-class citizens rely on the services of the working class to clean their houses, teach their children, and protect their substantial private property. Lower-class citizens depend on the rich for their livelihood. But notice that the only reason why there's something called an "upper class" in Neptune is that there's another group, labeled "the lower class." And the reverse holds as well—there can be no "lower" without an "upper" to compare it to.

Binary opposition is a common way of creating social categories or labels. All too often, however, one of the opposites is assigned a higher value and is regarded as the default, dominant, or privileged category, superior to its opposite. For example, the French feminist philosopher Simone de Beauvoir (1908–1986) argued that the male has been traditionally regarded as the default representation of people in general ("humanity is male"), while the female was considered something different from and less than a man. "[I]f I wish to define myself," she explained, "I must first of all say: 'I am a woman.' … A man never begins by presenting himself as an individual of a certain sex; it goes without saying that he is a man."[2] The two terms are not symmetrical or equal in any way.

This particular form of duality, in which one category is privileged as normal while its opposite is considered deviant or lacking, is what thinkers such as Beauvoir refer to when they speak of creating an Other. "Othering" represents our tendency to declare one category more desirable or acceptable than its opposite. Othering is binary opposition's natural sibling. They both categorize the world by comparing similar entities and then defining them through their differences; thus a woman is defined as a human being who *is not* male. But, unlike a neutral opposite, an Other is generally stigmatized and, in some cases, oppressed by the more powerful social group.

Othering is alive and well in Neptune, since residents of the town are defined through their relationships with the privileged inner circle of Neptune's rich and powerful. Working for the rich—or even being a person of modest means who is independently employed, like Keith Mars, or a public employee, like Sheriff Don Lamb—makes you inferior in spite of your belonging to the numerical majority. That's because the rich are also powerful. The 09-ers consider themselves the real Neptunians, while everyone else is an Other. But economic class doesn't provide the only criterion for binary opposition that structures Neptune society, nor are the non-rich the only group that gets defined as the Other.[3]

"How Do You People Not Make Yourselves Sick?"

In the unaired opening sequence from the extended DVD version of the pilot episode, we are first introduced to Veronica Mars during an encounter with the PCH Bike Club and its leader, Eli "Weevil" Navarro. It's a scene that's loaded with stereotypical racial and gender power dynamics—a small blond girl surrounded by young Mexican American bikers, leather-clad and scowling, their engines growling, and the implicit threat of violence made clear. And yet, as is often the case in *Veronica Mars*, the scene plays out in unexpected fashion, Veronica gaining the upper hand and Weevil reluctantly agreeing to accept her assistance. Congratulations! You've just been introduced to the racial binary of Neptune, California.

The town with two classes is also the town with two major racial and ethnic groups: whites and Hispanics. The large Hispanic population makes sense in light of the show's setting. California has one of the largest populations of Mexican immigrants in the United States. And, just as the class division in Neptune is marked by hostility and suspicion, so too is conflict an ever present aspect of the town's race relations, the clash between the two racial groups being highlighted in various plotlines throughout the series.

Moreover, race and class divisions coincide in Neptune, as exemplified in the conflict between Weevil and Logan Echolls, the most prominent member of the privileged, rich, and white 09-er Neptune teenagers. In the episode "Credit's Where Credit's Due," Weevil and three members of his PCH Biker crew crash an 09-er party, which prompts an exchange of insults between Logan and Weevil. Weevil refers to his lack of golfing privileges at Tory Pines, while Logan sarcastically compliments Weevil's grandmother's cleaning talents, throwing in a racial slur ("spic and span") for good measure. This encounter not only under-scores the racial tensions in Neptune but also shows us how those tensions intersect with the class issues prominently featured on the show. And the relationship between racial groups is no more symmetrical than that between economic classes. One is privileged, while the other is, well, the Other.

In "The Girl Next Door," English teacher Tom Daniels calls out Logan and Weevil for squabbling with each other during an exam. After giving both Logan and Weevil zero marks, Daniels is treated to Logan's muttered comment about his sex life. Daniels responds: "You know, the glow of your father's wealth and celebrity may be enough to sustain you through high school, Mr. Echolls, but do you know what it will get you in the real world?" Logan clasps his hands together and looks heavenward: "Please say 'high school English teacher.' Please say 'high school English teacher.'" Daniels isn't amused. Weevil, however, can't help laughing at Logan's disrespectful joke, which earns him a class-based insult from Daniels ("I wonder if you'll find Mr. Echolls so amusing ten years from now, when you're pumping his gas")—along with a stint in detention together with Logan. Though Daniels's obvious disdain for both young men makes him appear neutral in this little dustup between Logan and Weevil, he's actually taken a side in their greater social conflict. His insults imply that, regardless of how much Logan's status may diminish after high school, Weevil will still be his inferior. Daniels has aligned himself with the rich and powerful of Neptune by othering Weevil as an inveterate underachiever.

During detention, Weevil confronts Logan about his privileged status. "How do you people not make yourselves sick?" he asks. "I mean, it's like you walk on water in this school. For what? It's nothing that you do. All that matters is who your parents are and the zip code your mom shot you out in." Logan responds to this excellent summary of the source of Neptune's power differential by offering to donate to the "United Latino Pain-in-the-Ass Fund" if Weevil will just "shut the hell up."

These exchanges illustrate how Logan and Weevil deal with each other as representatives of their respective class and racial groups—and not as individuals. Logan's sense of superiority in relation to Weevil—and to non-09-ers generally—is a running theme in the series, as is Weevil's resentment of Logan's unearned privilege. The latter is prominently displayed when Logan is accused of killing a PCH Biker, Felix Toombs. Weevil tells Veronica that Logan got away with this murder "because he's rich and he's white" ("Normal Is the Watchword"). Though Weevil was wrong about Logan's guilt, he was certainly right about the benefits of being rich and white in Neptune.

"Why Do You Care So Much for That Skinny Negro Anyway?"

While Neptune is rife with class conflict, racial animosity is typically, though not exclusively, reserved for interactions between whites and Hispanics. The antagonism between these two groups creates the dominant binary opposition that characterizes race relations in this town. White Americans are the most prevalent group, in a recurring "guy in the background opening his locker" sort of way. The second largest group is that of Hispanics. But there are obviously more than just two races in Neptune. There are also African American citizens, along with the occasional Asian American teacher and Arab American vandalism victim ("Un-American Graffiti"). However, the racial makeup of Neptune doesn't necessarily show us how race is lived by its citizens. Race doesn't mean the same thing for every racial group. For some it's a defining factor, dominating their lives in a way that other minorities don't experience.

Mr. Wu, an Asian American science teacher at Neptune High, is forced to endure racist insults from Logan and Dick Casablancas, but this isolated incident doesn't seem to indicate any ongoing racial tension between Asians and whites in Neptune ("I Am God"). The same can be said about the experience of the Krimani family. Nothing suggests that the "terrorist" graffiti scrawled across their restaurant have been a regular occurrence since they moved to the town ("Un-American Graffitti"). And, though Madison Sinclair accuses the African American character Jackie Cook of "lurking" around a stolen moneybox—which prompts Jackie's riposte: "You mean standing while black?"—it isn't obvious that Madison's remark was intended as a racial slight and, even if it was, it represents yet another isolated incident. These infrequent conflicts involving other races are vastly outnumbered by the constant animosity between whites and Hispanics in Neptune.

Racial conflict in the United States has historically been framed in terms of black versus white. Given the centuries-long enslavement and subjugation of African Americans, it's not hard to understand why. The majority of laws and court cases prohibiting racial discrimination were originally designed to protect African Americans, although they apply to everyone. The struggles of other oppressed groups are often compared to and understood by analogy with the historical struggles of African Americans for civil rights. For example, the right of undocumented (and, in the specific case, predominantly Mexican) children to attend public school was established by using laws historically created to protect the rights of African Americans.[4]

Neptune's racial binary is similar to that of the United States in general, but there the site of the conflict is typically white versus Hispanic rather than white versus black. In other words, in Neptune racial conflict is framed in terms of brown versus white. Despite the presence of other races, the experience of race as a source of conflict and othering is reserved for the Hispanic population. Carmen Ruiz explains to Veronica that Latinos who date whites or join honor society are called "coconuts": people brown on the outside and white on the inside. When Veronica apologizes for the insult, Carmen shrugs it off with the remark "you didn't make the rules" ("Versatile Toppings"). These rules are designed to maintain the racial binary between whites and Hispanics. Other interracial relationships, such as those between Wallace and Jane Kuhne or between Alicia Fennel and Keith Mars, carry no such repercussions.[5]

"I Suddenly Feel Like I'm in a Scene from *The Outsiders*"

Wallace Fennel is first seen taped naked to a flagpole, with the word "Snitch" written across his chest ("Pilot"). He's being punished for tripping an alarm at the Sac N Pac, where he observed two members of the PCH Bike Club shoplifting during his work shift, so he obviously won't be going for a joy ride with that group any time soon. His first and best friend in town is Veronica, a loner and a social pariah in the eyes of the privileged 09-ers, so he definitely isn't going to bond with the rich and powerful. Also—and perhaps more obviously—he's African American, so he doesn't belong to either of the dominant racial groups in Neptune. When Logan and Weevil clash in the final scene of the "Pilot," it's not for nothing that he says: "I suddenly feel like I'm in a scene from *The Outsiders*." He really is on the outside looking in, as he watches the leaders of two dominant Neptune groups battle it out over a broken window. So, if Wallace is outside the racial binary, where exactly do he and other similarly situated Neptunians fit?

Racial minorities in Neptune are generally isolated within the white majority of the town. The African American families that we see on the show are small, with only one or two children. The friendships that we see African Americans form are typically with whites, as showcased by the bond between Wallace and Veronica. Jackie's brief friendship with Cora Briggs is a rare exception and is soon replaced by a closer bond with Veronica. Following his encounter with Logan and Weevil, Tom Daniels is seen walking with a white co-worker who's given him a ride to work ("The Girl Next Door"). Alicia Fennel becomes romantically involved with Keith Mars, while Mr. Wu and African American teacher Mallory Dent are seen interacting primarily with their white students. The Krimanis appear to be the only

Arab American family in town. We don't see the Krimanis and Fennels bonding over dinner, nor do we see Jackie and Mr. Wu hammering out a chemistry project after school. Why is it that the non-Hispanic minorities in Neptune seem to form their important relationships with whites? And why are they for the most part culturally indistinguishable from the white majority?

Philosopher Pierre Bourdieu's (1930–2002) concept of "cultural capital" helps us to answer that question. Cultural capital consists of habits, abilities, and characteristics that allow an individual to succeed or be accepted by society.[6] Bourdieu developed this concept in order to explain discrepancies in the achievement levels of young schoolchildren from different social backgrounds. He argued that certain cultural habits are actually valuable predictors of success. Proper speech is one example of a cultural habit that Bourdieu believes can become a type of capital or currency to be parlayed into an improved financial or social position.[7] That's why Logan's mockery of Weevil's bad grammar in "The Girl Next Door" is such an effective method of demoralization, especially since they're in the process of taking an English exam. The more cultural capital you obtain, the easier it is for you to function and succeed within your culture. Whites are Neptune's dominant racial group, so it isn't surprising that African Americans, Asian Americans, and Arab Americans would tend to socialize with them, since hanging out with white people at the lunch table or taking a white date to prom could help them acquire the cultural habits they need if they are to succeed.

The members of Neptune's Hispanic population, however, have their own cultural habits, such as mixing Spanish with English and dating exclusively within their community. Some Neptune Hispanics, like Carmen Ruiz or Marco Oliveres, obtain cultural capital outside this community, through interracial dating and friendships. However, opportunities to interact across racial lines are limited for many other members of the Hispanic community. Weevil is surrounded by his extended family—grandmother, niece, cousin, and uncle—plus his friends and the PCH Bikers, all of whom share the same racial background. His friendship with Veronica Mars and his romantic relationship with Lilly Kane are different from his typical social interactions, which is one reason why his relationship with Veronica has such a rough beginning. It's that white versus brown oppositional binary at work.

What happens when someone is unable or unwilling to obtain the cultural capital valued by the dominant racial group? In Neptune, it means that there is little opportunity to improve one's social position; people are confined to the roles associated with the oppositional relationship of the racial binary. Consequently, Hispanics in Neptune are often impoverished, employed as domestics, and have frequent encounters with law enforcement. For example, Weevil and Logan, the two poster children for Neptune's racial binary, maintain their relative positions until the end of the series. Logan is well on his way to graduating from college and maintaining his privileged status, while Weevil works as a janitor at the same university where Logan studies, and he's still seeking Veronica's help for his frequent legal troubles.

In contrast to Weevil, Wallace acquires cultural capital through personal relationships, scholastic achievements, and largely color-blind interactions. He becomes popular in high school through his athletic ability, despite his affiliation with the unpopular Veronica Mars. His prowess on the basketball court also gets him a full scholarship to attend college, the ultimate provider of equal opportunity, further priming him for success in life. His race is a benign factor, similar to Veronica's hair color. Veronica's blonde-ness is often played for laughs, due to the mismatch between the blonde stereotype and her obvious intellect. Wallace's race is also a source of jest. According to a popular stereotype, being black means being cool. Wallace often refers to his race as a way to associate himself with this cliché. He shrugs off Veronica's attempt to make him look nerdy as a futile attempt to suppress his "pimp juice" ("The Wrath of Con"). He also explains his failure to master hacky sack by deeming it a "white man's sport" and "the final arena of unquestioned white domination" ("Welcome Wagon"). Obviously, Wallace's race is relevant only when it's funny. There are no seething racial tensions between him and other citizens of Neptune, either white or Hispanic, only a vague acknowledgment of differences that are no more important than his hair or eye color. Arguably this isn't very realistic, but it offers a hopeful glimpse of what racial relations *could* some day be.

Other minorities in Neptune also joke about their difference. Mr. Wu, for instance, explains to Veronica that "not all well-dressed, articulate, detailed-oriented men are gay. Some are just Asian" ("I Am God"). But, while the interactions between minority characters and other citizens of Neptune are generally colorblind or acknowledged in amiable ways, Neptune's racial binary remains firmly intact.

Mea Culpa

So how wrong was I to dismiss *Veronica Mars* as more of the same network material that turns a blind eye to issues of race? Given the explicit presence of racial divisions and conflict in the show, I was completely off base. But sometimes that's a good thing. Exploring the racial binary of Neptune allows us to look more closely at the role of race in our society. That's something that's been made increasingly hard to do by the growing belief that we've entered a postracial era where racial categories have become meaningless. Dissecting race relations and highlighting differences aren't very popular things to do in a post-Barack Obama world. When racial discrimination is illegal and a black man can become president of the United States, what's the point of dwelling on a subject that has historically caused so much pain and sown so much animosity in people's lives?

The point is that race is still a part of our lives. We've done away with racially segregated bathrooms and restrictions on interracial marriage, but the impact of those discriminatory laws is still felt. Moreover, the divisive "othering" mentality that spawned them persists. It's important not to forget that. That's why it's salutary to watch characters like Logan and Weevil stubbornly playing their respective roles to their predictable endings. And it's also good to see characters like Wallace, who complicate clear-cut racial divisions and provide a surprising glimpse into the methods of social mobility. It makes this cynical African American viewer grateful to have her experience as part of a racial binary acknowledged and handled so admirably on primetime network television.

In the words of Veronica: "This is a beautiful thing" ("The Bitch Is Back").

Notes

1. See Ferdinand de Saussure, *Course in General Linguistics*, trans. Wade Baskin, ed. Charles Bally and Albert Sechehaye, collab. Albert Reidlinger (New York: Philosophical Library, 1959).
2. Simone de Beauvoir, *The Second Sex*, trans. H. M. Parshley (London: Lowe & Brydon Printers, 1956), xxi–xxii.
3. For more on social class in Neptune, see Chapter 1 in this volume, by William Irwin.
4. *Plyer v. Doe*, 457 US 202 (1982).
5. One exception is the secret relationship between the Arab American Amira Krimani and the Jewish American Jason Cohen ("Un-American Graffiti"). Rashad Krimani, Amira's father, disapproves of the union because of Jason's background, but he reluctantly agrees to meet Jason after delivering a loving speech about the American tradition of inclusion. However, aside from the fact that isolated instances of racial conflict wouldn't impact the dominance of the racial binary, the conflict in this case is arguably based more on religious differences rather than on race or ethnicity.
6. Pierre Bourdieu, "The Forms of Capital," originally published in J. Richardson, ed., *Handbook of Theory and Research for the*

Sociology of Education (New York, Greenwood), 241–258, Eitan Berglas School of Economics, http://econ.tau.ac.il/papers/publicf/ Zeltzer1.pdf, pp. 49–53 (accessed August 16, 2013).

7. Pierre Bourdieu, "Cultural Reproduction and Social Reproduction," in Richard Brown, ed., *Knowledge, Education and Cultural Change: Papers in the Sociology of Education* (London: Harpers and Row, Barnes and Noble Import Division, 1973), pp. 71–84.

Part II

VERONICA MARS IS A TRIPLE THREAT—GIRL, TEENAGER, AND PRIVATE DETECTIVE

INVESTIGATING THE WORLD OF *NOIR*

Breaking Bad in Neptune
How "Cool Guys" Become Psychopaths

George A. Dunn

"I track down the bad guys, call you, you make the bust," Veronica Mars tells Deputy Jerry Sacks. "You know what that makes everyone, Sacks? A winner" ("Welcome Wagon"). And the "wins" keep coming for Veronica, due to a seemingly never-ending stream of bad guys: murderers, rapists, thieves, dognappers, blackmailers, vandals, and scam artists of every stripe. Moving through a *noir* landscape of crime, violence, and corruption, our cynical teen detective is seldom wanting for bad guys to track down.

Of course, it isn't just the hooligans and ne'er-do-wells lurking in the shadows who fall on the wrong side of the moral equation in Neptune. Those in authority are, as a rule, not much better. Good old Deputy Sacks works for a sheriff's department that had an interesting arrangement with the Seventh Veil strip club. Officers would turn a blind eye to the club's "rather lax ID policy" in exchange for a little action in the squad car outside the club ("Pilot"). The department is headed by the corrupt Sheriff Don Lamb, who's not above using blackmail to extort a campaign contribution from his constituent Terrence Cook ("Versatile Toppings"). And then there's Woody Goodman, one

Veronica Mars and Philosophy: Investigating the Mysteries of Life (Which is a Bitch Until You Die), First Edition. Edited by George A. Dunn.
© 2014 John Wiley & Sons, Inc. Published 2014 by Wiley Blackwell.

of the town's most prominent citizens, owner of Neptune's professional baseball team, and a successful candidate for Balboa county supervisor. On the side, he's a double-crossing, chlamydia-transmitting child molester ("Not Pictured"). Even the principal at Veronica's school has a scandalous past, having once impregnated a student and then dumped his infant daughter at the school prom to cover his crime ("My Mother, the Fiend"). Veronica's closest friends and allies aren't exactly angels either: Duncan Kane orders a hit on Aaron Echolls ("Not Pictured"), Eli "Weevil" Navarro arranges the demise of Eduardo "Thumper" Orozco ("Plan B"), and, as for Logan Echolls, he may not have killed anyone yet, but with his anger management problems it may just be a matter of time.

In short, Veronica inhabits a world that's swarming with bad or, at best, morally ambiguous characters, a world that's perhaps more like our own than many of us would care to admit. As viewers of *Veronica Mars*, we may be so busy piecing together clues to solve the more immediate mysteries at hand— Who's responsible for the bus crash? Who's at Veronica's door?—that we seldom take notice of the much deeper puzzle that looms beneath the surface of the show's steady procession of crimes and scandals: *What's with everyone in Neptune breaking bad?* Or, more generally, why do people—not just in Neptune but everywhere—do so many bad things? That's a mystery that has bedeviled philosophers and other sleuths for millennia. It's a tough nut to crack. But, like Veronica, we're a whole lot tougher. So let's get cracking.

My Big Fat Sociology Experiment

Dr. Kinny, the Hearst College sociology professor, has an advantage over us philosophers: he gets to conduct his experiments in moral psychology with real people. As most students who have ever taken an ethics class know, philosophers are inordinately fond of what we call "thought experiments," where we outline various nerve-wracking scenarios, typically some matter of life or death, and then ask our students: "What would you do?" When students ask me why I put them through these mental ordeals, I patiently explain that there's just too much university paperwork that has to be completed before they'll let me do *real* experiments with my students. And then there are all those pesky liability issues that arise when, for instance, innocent people get pushed in the path of runaway trolleys. (Don't ask.)[1]

Luckily for Dr. Kinny, he isn't hamstrung like me. He's able to enlist—bribe, actually—a group of freshman sociology students, including Wallace Fennel and Logan, to participate in a simulated enactment of one of philosophy's all-time favorite "thought experiments": the ticking time bomb scenario. Encamping his students in an unused dorm that has been converted into a mock prison, Dr. Kinny divides them up into two groups, "guards" and "prisoners," announcing to the former: "A bomb will go off in 48 hours. You must get the location of the bomb from a prisoner to ensure the safety of innocent people" ("My Big Fat Greek Rush Weekend"). And, as if saving lives isn't incentive enough, the guards will be rewarded with exemption from writing a 20-page term paper if they can successfully extract the information in the allotted time. The prisoners, in turn, will be exempted if they can keep the location secret.

Philosophers have often posed this ticking time bomb scenario as a thought experiment designed to test our intuitions about if and when the use of torture might be justified. But Dr. Kinny is less concerned with the morality of torture than with figuring out how people can be induced to do it. And he's especially eager to confirm his hypothesis that, under the right conditions, even ordinary, seemingly decent people can be brought to do "cruel and awful and unconscionable" things. His class lecture highlights one example of shocking cruelty committed by otherwise ordinary folks that was still fresh in everyone's mind at the time: the torture and humiliation inflicted on Iraqi prisoners by

American soldiers at the notorious Abu Ghraib facility in 2003–2004.

Showing a picture of an American guard abusing an Iraqi prisoner, Dr. Kinny asks the class: "Who of you saw this photo from Abu Ghraib and thought, 'I would never do that to another human being'?" When almost every hand in the room goes up, he casually breaks the news that they're all in the grips of a self-congratulatory delusion. The prison experiment is designed to drive this point home, to reveal just how susceptible these good students are to bad environmental influences and how easily they can be lured into doing bad things, despite their good opinion of themselves.

Most neighborhoods in Neptune are a lot swankier than the simulated prison on the Heart campus; they have ample creature comforts and generally pleasant surroundings. Even so, just like that dark prison, this sunshiny town seems to offer a great environment for bringing out the worst in people. Philosophers have traditionally looked at factors like temperament and personality traits in their search for the causes of human wickedness. Maybe we should have been looking at zip codes.

"Despite Popular Opinion, You Really Can't Beat the Truth Out of Someone"

Or so Veronica tells Logan when he offers to accompany her to meet Sondra Bolan, the woman who claims to have witnessed Lynn Echolls's suicide ("Mars vs. Mars"). But perhaps you *can* emotionally brutalize someone to the point that he tells you what you want to know. That, at least, is what the smirking, sadistic "guard" Rafe sets out to do to Samuel Horshack, the emotionally fragile "prisoner" whom Rafe identifies right off the bat as the weak link. Rafe dives into his role with gusto: he engages in belittling, name-calling, and ethnic slurs; he follows Horshack into the bathroom, leans over his shoulder, and torments him about his bashful kidneys, making it impossible for him to urinate; and he ridicules Horshack mercilessly when, as would be expected for someone who's been prevented from using the bathroom, Horshack wets his pants. And yet, outside this mock prison environment, Rafe is, at least according to Horshack, "a cool guy."

Can someone be both a "cool guy" and a gleeful, psychopathic torturer? That's precisely the conclusion that psychologist Philip Zimbardo drew from the Stanford prison experiment (SPE) that he conducted at Stanford University back in 1971, one of the most famous—or notorious—studies in the history of psychology and the real-life model for Dr. Kinny's fictional research. Zimbardo wanted to understand the roots of human cruelty and wickedness. And, like his fictional counterpart Dr. Kinny, Zimbardo hypothesized that situational and environmental factors played a much larger role in shaping human behavior than had previously been appreciated. While many other psychologists were ready to chalk up the presence of evil in the world to the miscreant behavior of a "few bad apples"—that small but noxious gallery of blackhearted rogues that includes ruthless criminals like the Fitzpatricks, corrupt cops like Don Lamb, and conscienceless CEOs like Richard "Big Dick" Casablancas—Zimbardo thought that we should look instead at the "apple barrels" where those scoundrels flourish. Could it be that bad behaviors were the product of social institutions that could, under the right conditions, bring the dark side of human nature to the surface even in people who might be pretty "cool guys" in other settings? "Although you probably think of yourself as having a consistent personality across time and space, that is likely not to be true," Zimbardo wrote in a book describing his experiment.[2] Whether you're good or bad may depend on the situation you find yourself in.

Zimbardo created the SPE as a way to test his hypothesis that we're all capable of appallingly evil acts, given the right set of circumstances—and what could be better suited to nurture our worst instincts than a prison setting where guards and prisoners are pitted against each other, one group having absolute power and the other being entirely at the former's mercy. The philosophically minded novelist Milan Kundera once wrote: "True human goodness, in all its purity and freedom, can come to the fore only when its recipient has no power."[3] This makes sense when you consider that otherwise your acts of kindness never entirely escape the suspicion that they're just ploys to put someone in your debt. But the flip side of this insight is that power itself can be a potent conscience-suppressant that can lead us to commit some truly despicable acts. Time and time again, Veronica has uncovered the corruptions of power at the headwaters of the sleaze that runs through Neptune, flowing from mansions, corporate offices, and the sheriff's department as often as it does from the River Styx.

Zimbardo's study, like Kinny's, lends considerable support to the old adage that power corrupts. Within an extraordinarily short period of time, the guards began abusing the prisoners, devising highly creative ways of demeaning and demoralizing them, including various forms of sexual humiliation. But the study also turned up another result, one that the experiment at Hearst also replicates. Not all of Zimbardo's guards were actively engaged in brutalizing the prisoners, but even those who didn't personally dish out the brutality were complicit in the abuse, if only by looking the other way. Similarly, though clearly appalled by the zest with which Rafe persecutes Horshack, Wallace never intervenes to stop it beyond issuing one mild protest of "Hey, man." And in due course even Wallace, usually so kindhearted and gentle, is reveling in his power as a guard, taunting the prisoners about the decidedly unappetizing excuse for a dinner they're being fed. For a parallel to this complicity of "good" people in villainous acts, we need look no further than the night of Shelly Pomeroy's party, when even those like Casey Grant, who weren't directly involved in taking advantage of Veronica's inebriated state, were still guilty of standing by and letting the abuse happen ("A Trip to the Dentist").

Zimbardo's prison experiment differed from Dr. Kinny's in a few significant respects, though: Zimbardo didn't assign the guards the task of extracting a piece of information from the prisoners—he simply charged them with the responsibility to maintain "law and order"—and the ordeal was supposed to last a whole two weeks rather than just 48 hours. After only six days, though, the SPE had to be ended, so quickly did the guards turn sadistic, so extreme was their cruel, degrading, and dehumanizing treatment of their prisoners, and so intense was the prisoners' emotional distress. Some prisoners were so psychologically broken that they became like zombies, obeying every whim of their captors without question. When we consider both the sadism of the guards and the suffering and ensuing submissiveness of the prisoners, Dr. Kinny's experiment at Hearst College can only be described as "SPE lite."

There's this difference as well: all the participants in Zimbardo's SPE were screened through a battery of personality tests and background surveys to weed out those with existing psychological problems. These were seemingly healthy and well-adjusted young men (all the participants in the SPE were males), not personalities whom we might suspect of a predisposition toward either sadism or extreme submissiveness. In other words, they weren't a bunch of Rafes and Horshacks, who appear to have arrived at Dr. Kinny's mock prison already heavily laden with a host of psychological issues that would have probably got them excluded from Zimbardo's SPE. Those two guys were made for each other. Or at least their respective personality disorders apparently were.

The Axis of Mercer

Upon learning that Wallace has volunteered for Dr. Kinny's prison experiment, resident advisor Moe Slater divulges that he "did the experiment last year." Sinking for a moment into wistful reverie, he describes the experience as "intense" and "life-changing" ("My Big Fat Greek Rush Weekend"). Indeed! "Life-changing" may be the mother of all understatements! Subsequent revelations lead us to surmise that it was during his life-changing prison weekend that Moe, assigned the role of a prisoner, first formed his twisted bond with Mercer Hayes, one of his guards. At least that's what's suggested by several clues that emerge after Veronica uncovers Mercer's identity as the Hearst College rapist. While hiding from Mercer in Moe's room, Veronica spots a photograph of the pair together, in which Moe is wearing the striped shirt used in Dr. Kinny's experiment to denote prisoners and Mercer is dressed in the shirt of a guard. A short time later, after Veronica brings a hammer down on Moe's foot and causes him to howl in pain, Mercer yells in Moe's face: "Stop blubbering, prisoner!" Mercer follows up the verbal rebuke with a hard backhanded blow to the face of the "prisoner," who is now cowering on his knees, like a frightened supplicant ("Spit & Eggs").

Clearly the pattern of dominance and submission established in prison between the arrogant and sadistic Mercer and his whimpering whipping boy Moe has become the template of their subsequent relationship, as Moe obediently helps Mercer to indulge his other outlet for antisocial urges: raping and humiliating women. When we hear about Rafe and Horshack later in the semester, there are indications they've fallen into a similar relationship of abusive codependency: what begins with Horshack taking notes for Rafe when the latter is absent from class during the week after the experiment ("My Big Fat Greek Rush Weekend") escalates into Horshack helping Rafe cheat by taking his test for him ("Hi, Infidelity!"). It would be rash to conclude that the next chapter in this warped relationship will see Horshack helping Rafe to commit a string of felonies, but their ongoing prisoner–guard bond *does* bear a disturbing resemblance to the toxic Mercer–Moe compact.

Should we therefore conclude that Dr. Kinny is ultimately responsible for the rapes on the Hearst campus, since he was the one who paired up a psychopath with his toady? (And possibly did it for two years in a row—what are the odds?) No; but the situation does suggest that he should probably have screened his participants more carefully. And it also calls into question the validity of his results, if those participants included young men who may have already had a taste for hurting others. After all, the point of such an experiment is to demonstrate, in Zimbardo's words, "the potentially toxic impact of bad systems and bad situations in making good people behave in pathological ways that are alien to their nature."[4] You can't really draw that conclusion if you start with characters like Mercer—and to a lesser degree Rafe—who undoubtedly contributed a lot of their own already toxic personality to making the situation as bad as it got. Could his participation in the experiment have been the "life-changing" event that pushed Mercer over the line, changing him from a merely arrogant and cruel college kid into a full-blown psychopath, who regards others as having value only to the extent that they can be used and exploited by him? Maybe. We'd need to consult an expert on the etiology of psychopathy about that. Even so, Mercer looks like the type who had probably been skirting that line for some time already.

But, even if we can't assign Dr. Kinny any blame for what Mercer did *after* the experiment, the professor is certainly responsible for any and all of the humiliation, degradation, dehumanization, and psychological torment that he subtly encouraged his students to inflict on each other in the course of those prison weekends. As in the SPE, in Dr. Kinny's experiment there were cameras filming everything. Dr. Kinny tells his students that they'll "be monitored at all times." So we need to imagine this dedicated seeker of knowledge sitting in his office, taking careful notes while riveted to a screen that displays Rafe dishing out verbal abuse and intimidation, laughing at Horshack's humiliation after the latter wets himself, and then locking him in a small, dark janitor's closet when Horshack defies the command not to change into dry clothes. No doubt, Dr. Kinny was treated to a similar—and possibly even more depraved—spectacle of cruelty the year before, when Mercer was the star of the show.

And so Dr. Kinny's research forces us to face a couple of uncomfortable questions. First, is the suffering of these student-prisoners, not to mention the moral corruption of these student-guards, an acceptable tradeoff for whatever knowledge is gained through this sort of research? I would say no. And that leads to the second question: What kind of dirt must Dr. Kinny have on the members of the research ethics committee at Hearst College that could have *possibly* got them to sign off on something like this? There's a mystery worthy of Veronica's sleuthing skills. Seriously, *this* is why we philosophers stick to thought experiments.

"Haven't Thought of You Lately at All"

The SPE is often cited as an example of the sort of study that couldn't be repeated today because it fails to meet the standards established by numerous ethical codes. Reflecting on the SPE decades later, Zimbardo himself was more than a little horror-struck at his own complicity in the evil he deliberately unleashed and allowed to continue—even after he could no longer ignore the severity of the psychological distress it was causing. The experiment was ended after only six days, more than a week ahead of schedule, only because Zimbardo's colleague Christina Maslach witnessed firsthand what was going on inside the prison and told him forthrightly: "What you are doing to those boys is a terrible thing!"[5] Sometimes even researchers in moral psychology need others to serve as an ersatz conscience when their own eyesight has been clouded by the seductions of power, as Zimbardo later acknowledged.

The power of the situation ran swiftly and deeply through most of those on this exploratory ship of human nature. Only a few were able to resist the situational temptations to yield to power and dominance while maintaining some semblance of morality and decency. Obviously, I was not among that noble class.[6]

As may be expected at a college located in Neptune, the Hearst faculty lacks anyone with the moral discernment and decency of Christina Maslach, who could have placed a much needed wakeup call to Dr. Kinny.

Can the SPE shed light on why evil is so prevalent in Neptune? Are the countless reprobates and villains who populate this *noir* town really just the product of bad situations that bring out the worst traits of otherwise good people? Would the Fitzpatricks have been model citizens in a different environment? And, instead of just tracking down "bad guys," should Veronica give more attention to reforming the bad systems that, according to Zimbardo, promote all this bad behavior? Certainly there must be some explanation for the fact that moral corruption has spread like a fungus through the town of Neptune, infecting every institution, from Neptune High School to Kane Software to the Balboa County Sheriff's Office. It's unlikely that there's something in the water. We should at least consider the possibility that the enormous discrepancies in power, wealth, and status in Neptune may have something to do with the fostering of attitudes like arrogance, a sense of entitlement, resentment, and envy that may blind some of the town's residents to the humanity of their fellow citizens and embolden whatever tendencies to antisocial behavior may be lurking in the shadowy corners of their hearts. The "town without a middle class" may have more in common with the faux prisons set up by Drs. Zimbardo and Kinny than appears at first blush.

But, although we face social pressures and temptations to break bad every day, many of us still find the wherewithal not to wander off the paths of decency into the dark alleys of iniquity.

What makes the difference? The philosopher Hannah Arendt (1906–1975), a German Jew who was forced to flee her homeland after the Nazis came to power, devoted much of her extraordinary intellectual life to unraveling this particular mystery. It was a mystery that hit as close to home for her as Lilly Kane's murder did for Veronica; for Arendt had not only witnessed up close the ascension to power of the Nazi Party, but had watched in horror and disbelief as many of her colleagues, including her mentor, the brilliant German philosopher Martin Heidegger (1889–1979), fell in lockstep with their hateful politics.

In seeking an explanation, Arendt didn't discount the role of social influences in turning seemingly good people to the dark side; but that didn't explain why some people were immune to those forces while others, including some of Germany's greatest intellectuals, succumbed. The conclusion she drew was that the chief cause of so many people's fall into complicity with evil "was not stupidity but a curious, quite authentic inability to think."[7]

> Inability to think is not stupidity; it can be found in highly intelligent people, and wickedness is hardly its cause, if only because thoughtlessness as well as stupidity are much more frequent phenomena than wickedness. The trouble is that no wicked heart, a relatively rare phenomenon, is necessary to cause great evil.[8]

The most common source of moral evil, according to Arendt, is the ubiquitous tendency of people to act without giving much thought to the consequences or significance of their actions. Serious moral reflection has an annoying habit of getting in the way of other things we want to do, like gratifying our desires and fitting in with others. That's why we have such a strong incentive to ignore the reproaches of conscience or to try to rationalize them away. And that's why Zimbardo needed Christina Maslach.

Consider the despicable Woody Goodman, who by molesting boys on his Little League team inadvertently set in motion a tragic sequence of events that culminated in a bus full of Neptune High students plunging off a cliff. When Keith Mars takes Woody into custody, the excuses come zipping out of his mouth like fastballs: "That's not how it was. It wasn't that way at all. Those boys … if you knew their fathers, how they ignored them, mistreated them. They needed someone. I listened to them. I cared about them" ("Not Pictured"). It's as though he had been rehearsing these rationalizations in his mind for years—and he undoubtedly had. Mercer also has ways of rationalizing his actions. "I'm just taking what you would have happily given," he evilly monologues into the ear of the girl who he thinks will be his next victim ("Spit & Eggs"). And even bush-league bully Rafe seems to have persuaded himself that he's simply taking the experiment "seriously" ("My Big Fat Greek Rush Week"). Excuses like these are beyond flimsy, but they can do a good enough job of keeping conscience at bay, as long as the wrongdoer never actually stops to *think* about how pathetic they really are.

From Arendt's perspective, the foremost cause of evil in Neptune (and elsewhere) is neither the *noir* environment that shapes behavior nor some inscrutable darkness that dwells in the human heart. It's our inability—or perhaps just unwillingness—to exercise independent moral judgment and to *think* seriously about our actions. In the end, the reason why we need Veronica and others like her to keep catching the bad guys is that most of us just don't *think* and consequently aren't very good at catching ourselves being bad.

Notes

1. Okay, since you asked, I'm referring to one of the most famous thought experiments in ethics: the trolley problem. Would you shove an innocent person in the path of a runaway trolley to save the lives of five other innocent people who are tied to the tracks up ahead?

Philippa Foot (1920–2010) was the first philosopher to propose a version of this quandary, but many other philosophers have since put their own spins on it. See Philippa Foot, *Virtues and Vices: And Other Essays in Moral Philosophy* (New York: Oxford University Press, 2003), 23.

2. Philip Zimbardo, *The Lucifer Effect: Understanding How Good People Turn Evil* (New York: Random House, 2007), 8.

3. Milan Kundera, *The Unbearable Lightness of Being: A Novel* (New York: Harper Perennial Classics, 2008), 313.

4. Zimbardo, *The Lucifer Effect*, 195.

5. Ibid., 171. Drs. Maslach and Zimbardo were later married.

6. Ibid., 173.

7. Hannah Arendt, *Responsibility and Judgment* (New York: Schoken Books, 2003), 159.

8. Ibid., 164.

5

Noir Neptune
Genre and Gender Bending in *Veronica Mars*

Daniel Wack

"I always thought our love was epic," Logan Echolls confesses to Veronica Mars, after drunkenly pulling her aside at the "alter-naprom" he's hosting ("Look Who's Stalking"). Though Logan is drunk and speaking hyperbolically, he's not just being sarcastic. In the moment, Veronica deflects his suggestion but she demonstrates that she appreciates his sincerity by appearing at his door the next morning to discuss it further. Though Logan speaks of "ruined lives" and "bloodshed," we suspect that by "epic" he means a struggle that overcomes obstacles and long odds to end happily. Given what they've both been through, he may hope that their love can redeem their world, make its suffering worth enduring, and transform their pain into a private happiness that delivers them from the corrupt and brutal world they've inherited.

The promise that Logan tenders—that the world he and Veronica inhabit is corrupt but can in some sense be redeemed for them through the power of their love and intimacy—parallels the promise that the *femme fatale* offers the protagonist in *film noir* movies. The possibility of a love strong enough to overcome the corruption and violence of the world of *film noir* is a

Veronica Mars and Philosophy: Investigating the Mysteries of Life (Which is a Bitch Until You Die), First Edition. Edited by George A. Dunn.
© 2014 John Wiley & Sons, Inc. Published 2014 by Wiley Blackwell.

promise that frequently seduces the protagonist, but it ultimately proves to be illusory—and often fatal. *Film noir*, first identified as a genre by a group of French critics interested in underappreciated Hollywood movies, is a notoriously wide-ranging genre, but many *film noirs* share three major elements with *Veronica Mars*:

- a corrupt world in which the story is set;
- a love interest, the *femme fatale*, who's a figure of sexual fascination and moral danger;
- and a protagonist who becomes obsessed with uncovering the truth whatever the costs.

Veronica Mars reimagines *film noir* for twenty-first-century television by transposing the *film noir* world into a class-riven high school, by making the main characters teenagers, and, most intriguingly, by switching the genders of the detective protagonist and of the love interest. The centerpiece of *Veronica Mars*'s transformation of the *film noir* paradigm is making the *noir* detective a teenage girl. The *femme fatale* (fatal woman) then becomes the *homme fatal* (fatal man)—Logan, whose hope of an epic love tempts both Veronica and the show's audience. But, as anyone familiar with *film noir* knows, the *femme fatale*, while holding forth the promise of transcendence, always in fact brings more trouble.

"A Town without a Middle Class"

In his landmark book on philosophy and film, *The World Viewed: Reflections on the Ontology of Film*, the philosopher Stanley Cavell argues that movie viewing involves grasping the moral nature of the world of the movie.[1] By watching a movie we come to understand what kinds of people inhabit its world and what kinds of action are possible for them, and thereby we recognize the world of the movie as being of a particular kind. In *film noir* the inhabitants of a corrupt world attempt to free themselves from bad situations but find themselves doomed to fail. *Noir* characters, in their attempt to escape their fate, often end up bringing it to pass. According to philosopher Robert Pippin, "in the best *noirs* we are presented not merely with a form of life shadowed, as a matter of historical fact, by a growing, shared, heightened sense of fatalism and alienation"—that is, a sense that the characters' fates have already been determined by previous actions whose consequences are inescapable—"but we see what is, in effect, a partially worked-out picture of what it would be to live in such a world."[2] According to Pippin, the characters of *film noir* share a sense that they live in a world in which their ability to act in meaningful ways is limited at best.

The world of *Veronica Mars* is marked by this sense of fate in two related ways. On the one hand, Neptune is riven by class differences. As Veronica says about her high school: "If you go here, your parents either are millionaires or your parents work for millionaires" ("Pilot"). Neptune High is split between the 09-ers—the rich kids, named from their "prestigious" zip code—and everyone else. Veronica's observation that Neptune is "without a middle class" makes it clear that this is a community without class mobility: one is either rich or poor. Moreover, the class status of students at Neptune High isn't a product of their own work or choice. Just as nobody chooses his or her own parents, nobody chooses his or her parents' finances. Veronica and her classmates are thus fated to share their parents' class status, along with the privileges or privations that status entails.

For example, Logan's profession of epic love to Veronica takes place at an "alternaprom" thrown by him and other 09-ers after the official prom was cancelled due to misbehavior on the part of some of the rich kids. Cancelling the prom was supposed to punish the student body as a whole, but, as Veronica points out, the rich kids can simply pay for the alternative prom and, because it's a private function, invite only their friends. Inherited class status, for which none of the students are responsible, shapes the lives of all the students at Neptune High: the rich are protected from the harmful consequences of their actions, while the poor suffer those consequences even when they're merely innocent bystanders. When Eli "Weevil" Navarro's grandmother is wrongfully accused of theft, the stability and security of the entire Navarro family is threatened ("Credit Where Credit's Due"). Meanwhile Dick Casablancas never faces any serious consequences for his chronic bullying and acts of vandalism.[3]

Neptune students aren't just fated to live with the consequences of their parents' finances, however. They often must also live with the consequences of their parents' *actions*. The prospects for Veronica and Duncan Kane's romance, for example, depend not just on their feelings for each other, but also on whether Duncan's father Jake Kane fathered Veronica during his affair with Lianne Mars, Veronica's mother. The sins of the parents in Neptune shape the lives of their children. The lives of Logan and Veronica, in particular, are lived in the shadow of their parents' actions. Veronica's status at Neptune High shifts dramatically when her father is recalled as sheriff. Logan, on the other hand, is protected by his father's wealth, but also shattered by his father's abuse. He must live with his father's murder of Lilly Kane, his own girl-friend, and with the suicide of his mother, Lynn Echolls, which was precipitated by Aaron Echolls's philandering. Both Logan and Veronica are fated to suffer the consequences of actions that were not theirs. For Logan, the promise of his love for Veronica is that it will redeem all that they've had to endure, all the suffering caused by the actions of others, and it will allow them to find happiness at last, in a transformed world.

"Fun? You Think I'm Having Fun?"

One of the most prominent figures in the original *film noirs* is an immensely attractive and seductive woman who entices the male protagonist into compromising or dangerous situations.

She consistently seems to be caught up with—or at least is discovered in close proximity to—crimes and other unsavory activities, though the nature of her involvement in these misdeeds may not be easy to determine. The French critics who identified the genre of *film noir* called this figure the *femme fatale*, the fatal woman. As already stated, one of the most radical and interesting ways in which *Veronica Mars* reimagines the genre is by reversing the genders between the *film noir*'s protagonist and its *femme fatale*. Logan fills the role of this captivating, seductive, and dangerous figure. In homage to his *film noir* roots, we may call him the *homme fatal*, the fatal man.

Like the *femme fatale*, Logan is regularly implicated in violent crimes without his own culpability ever being fully clear. He's an alibi for seedy characters such as Mercer Hayes ("Of Vice and Men"); he gets in a fight on the Coronado Bridge with the PCH-ers the night Felix Toombs is killed ("Normal is the Watchword"); he unwittingly sends Eduardo "Thumper" Orozco to his death by pushing the detonator that demolishes the stadium where Thumper is tied up ("Plan B"); and his girlfriend Lilly is murdered by his father. Often it seems that Logan's mere presence draws trouble and violence. Logan himself often feels guilty about this violence, even when he isn't directly responsible for it. He sometimes seems to be a conduit for violence. Almost any time there is violence and death in Neptune, Logan is involved, or at least in the general proximity.

But Logan's status as an object of sexual fascination and temptation deviates from the classic archetype. As *homme fatal* rather than *femme fatale*, he's not just the locus and the facilitator of violence; he himself is regularly violent, as when he dukes it out with Weevil in the bathroom ("My Mother, the Fiend"). Having absorbed years of physical abuse from his father, he redirects his rage outward. Sometimes, however, he's violent for romantic or chivalrous reasons, as when he smacks down Stosh "Piz" Piznarski ("Weevils Wobble but They Don't Go Down"), and later Gorya "Gory" Sorokin ("The Bitch is

Back"), in reaction to the sex tape of Veronica that had been circulating on campus. On another occasion he destroys a police car with a baseball bat in order to get arrested and placed in the same cell with Mercer Hayes. Having learned that Mercer, recently revealed as the Hearst College rapist, had assaulted Veronica, Logan is intent on hurting him in revenge ("Spit & Eggs").

The question of Logan's culpability in the violence around him is perhaps most pressing in the events at Shelly Pomeroy's party, when Cassidy "Beaver" Casablancas raped Veronica after she was drugged by ingesting a drink that Dick Casablancas had laced with GHB (Gamma-hydroxybutyric acid), intending to drug Madison Sinclair. Though not directly responsible for either the drugging or the rape, Logan is implicated in both deeds. In the first place, everyone at the party—but crucially Logan—could tell that Veronica was dangerously intoxicated, if not drugged, and therefore incapable of consenting to the sexual liberties people were taking with her. Yet neither Logan nor anyone else at the party intervened to help her. But Logan is even more implicated in Veronica's assault than most others. He supplied the GHB, was a leader in the group doing body shots off Veronica, and secretly drugged Duncan, which resulted in Duncan and Veronica having sex together.[4]

All the same, Logan remains the show's most compelling love interest for Veronica, a figure of fascination for both her and the audience. His responsibility for the violence around him often seems mitigated by his emotional devastation at the loss of his girlfriend and by his abusive home life. His ability to match wits with Veronica shows him to be her intellectual equal and, out of everyone in her life, he's closest to sharing her worldview, which comes out in their sarcastic banter with each other. That they are kindred spirits first becomes apparent when they cooperate to create a video tribute to Lilly that celebrates her exuberance and wildness rather than whitewashing her life, as her parents wished ("The Wrath of Con").

Given Logan's background, his dream of sharing an epic love with Veronica looks to be a dream of escaping the violence that swirls around him and of discovering a private world to which only the two of them will have access. His hope is that they don't have to occupy a fatalistic *noir* world that dooms them to an implacably violent destiny scripted for them in advance, but that they come instead to inhabit a world redeemed by their love. Much of Logan's allure for Veronica comes from his being a "bad boy" who can be saved by the strength of her love. But, in classic *film noir*, this promise of redemption through the power of love and intimacy—the promise that the *femme fatale* offers the *film noir* protagonist—is what draws the protagonist inexorably on, toward the doom that fate has prepared for him.

With Logan and Veronica, this promise of an epic love that can redeem doesn't lead directly to mutual doom, as it classically does in *film noir*. In part, this is because television is an open-ended medium, so whatever doom awaits the central characters must be deferred for as long as the series runs. But it also has something to do with the couple's being teenagers, with the girl as the protagonist and the boy as the figure of sexual fascination. In classic *film noir*, the *femme fatale* denotes the male fear of the power of female sexuality to paralyze and destroy. When the gender roles are flipped, Logan as the *fatal* remains a figure of sexual anxiety, but this anxiety largely arises from Veronica's own inability to trust others.[5] That Logan fills the role of the *homme fatal* in Veronica's world helps explain why their relationship doesn't succeed. Accepting Logan's promise of an epic love story would mean surrendering too much of the independence Veronica has won through the hard struggles that have taught her how to remain active and self-sufficient in a corrupt world suffused with a sense of fatalism.

"I Know All of This Because I Have Done Everything I Can to Get to the Truth"

The detective in *noir* movies is driven by the need to know, typically to learn the truth about a murder at the epicenter of a web of corruption that touches all aspects of the world of the movie. Learning the truth about this murder often means sacrificing the stability of the protagonist's world, precipitating a world-shattering disaster. In earlier *film noirs* such as *The Maltese Falcon* or *The Big Sleep*, the detective is hired by clients to solve a mystery. Over the course of his investigation, his personal investment in the case deepens as a result of his emotional connection with the *femme fatale*, as well as of the pride he takes in being able to discover the truth. Veronica, on the other hand, becomes a detective in response to her world's having already been shattered. She takes on clients from episode to episode, much as the earlier detectives did, but her commitment to detective work arises from her intimate personal need to know how and why her world was destroyed. From the pilot episode on, she dedicates herself to learning the truth about three events: her rape at Shelly Pomeroy's party, her mother's disappearance, and, of course, Lilly Kane's murder. Her desperate commitment to discovering the truth is expressly founded on the hope that the knowledge she gains will restore a semblance of order and justice to her world.

In her commitment to the truth, Veronica resembles a philosopher, a scientist, or a scholar—individuals dedicated to the truth, often at the expense of other things that they care about. Knowing the truth, on this view, is one of the most valuable things there are, something to be sought for its own sake. Furthermore, the truth sought by philosophers, scholars, and scientists is linked to impartiality, because what's true doesn't depend on any one person's point of view or way of thinking. Veronica certainly takes the truth to be a good thing; but she doesn't pretend that possessing knowledge is good in itself, or equally valuable for everyone. Indeed she suggests to Cindy "Mac" Mackenzie that she might *not* want to know the truth about her paternity ("Silence of the Lamb"). Veronica is well aware that, for her, discovering the truth is a personal quest that defines who she is. Because the truths she seeks are about the things that matter most to her, the knowledge she gains inevitably has practical consequences and demands some action in response. Accordingly, she refuses to learn the truth about her own paternity, fearing that it would threaten her self-understanding and disrupt her relationship with Keith Mars, whom she has always loved as her father ("Drinking the Kool-Aid"). "When I had the opportunity to learn my paternity, I chose blissful ignorance with a side of gnawing doubt," she says ("Silence of the Lamb").[6]

Even so, Veronica's dedication to learning the truth about what happened to Lilly, to her own family, and to herself the night of Shelly Pomeroy's party turns out to be more complicated than she initially thought. As she describes her mission in the opening episode's voiceover, learning the truth about these three events will be a force for justice and a way to restore the order that has been destroyed. She says about her mother's disappearance: "I will find out what really happened and I will bring this family back together again" ("Pilot"). But only the investigation into Lilly's murder has any real restorative effects, since learning that Aaron Echolls killed Lilly allows Veronica to say goodbye to her friend and to restore her father's reputation.

By contrast, learning the truth about how and why her family collapsed doesn't bring her family back together. In fact it's hard to imagine how it could. Veronica's search for the truth about what happened to her family seems to have been mostly a way to avoid acknowledging what she saw unfold. As long as she keeps investigating, she can postpone coming to terms with the fact that her mother is an alcoholic who abandoned her family because she couldn't handle the aftermath of Keith's losing his job as sheriff. Similarly, her commitment to learning what happened at Shelly's party is in part a way to avoid facing the fact that she was drugged and raped at a party attended by over one hundred of her classmates, none of whom intervened to help her. In both cases, Veronica wants a story that separates the good guys from the bad guys, imposes order on the world, and makes sense of events that otherwise appear to be senseless, chaotic, and cruel. Unfortunately things don't work that way in the *noir* world.

But if Veronica's dedication to the truth can never restore her world to its former order, then what does she get out of being a detective? She sometimes seems to regard her sleuthing as a source of connection with her father. But this means that, for Veronica, being a detective, far from restoring her world to its former order, actually provides a new way for her to order her world. Though she wins minor victories for justice from episode to episode, nothing she does can change the corrupt and disappointing nature of her world. However, being a detective does allow her to understand Neptune in all its guilty secrets, cynical motivations, and corrupt dealings. Learning these truths won't return her world to the way it used to be, but it will help her to find a new way forward, as she comes to know it as it is. The benefit for her is that she now has a way of being in the world that protects her from its disappointments, since she knows what to expect.

And that's why Logan's hope for an epic love with Veronica that will redeem their suffering and transform the nature of their world can't come to pass. For Logan, part of the appeal of this epic scenario undoubtedly stems from the fact that, in his imagined epic, he would assume the role of protector and rescuer of the damsel in distress. But that would require Veronica to trade in her active way of being for a more passive role in Logan's epic, submitting herself to his protection and depending on him to rescue her. In short, she would have to sacrifice her hard-won understanding of herself as someone who generates knowledge of the truth and brings order to her world. Given all that she has suffered and overcome, Veronica could never give up being a detective: it has become how she makes sense of her world and herself.

Notes

1. Stanley Cavell, *The World Viewed: Reflections on the Ontology of Film* (Cambridge, MA: Harvard University Press, 1979). For more on Cavell and on the conventions of *noir* fiction, see Chapter 16 in this volume, by James B. South.
2. Robert Pippin, *Fatalism in American Film Noir: Some Cinematic Philosophy* (Charlottesville, VA: University of Virginia Press, 2012), 12.
3. For more on how class status affects the lives of Neptune's residents, see Chapter 1 in this volume, by William Irwin.
4. For more on Logan's culpability on the night of Shelly's party, see Chapter 10 in this volume, by James Rocha and Mona Rocha.
5. For more on Veronica's inability to trust, see Chapter 9 in this volume, by Jon Robson.
6. For more on whether the truth is good in itself, see Chapter 13 in this volume, by Dereck Coatney.

6

"Don't Forget about Me, Veronica"
Time, Memory, and Mystery in *Veronica Mars*

Paul Hammond

The beachside community of Neptune is a place with a profound relationship to its own past. Veronica spends her entire junior year of high school haunted by recollections of her best friend, Lilly Kane, who was murdered the previous year. Veronica sees things that remind her of Lilly everywhere: at school, when driving in her car, and whenever she looks at Lilly's brother, Duncan Kane, who used to be Veronica's boyfriend. She's driven by the feeling that this history and the memory of her friend require something of her, that the past is unresolved and presents a problem that has to be figured out. When not attending to other urgent private investigator (PI) business, Veronica spends her time gathering clues and trying to piece together the real story of Lilly's death.

The past also haunts Veronica in the mystery of her mother's disappearance. Lianne Mars has been MIA ("missing in action") since soon after Lilly's murder. In addition, Veronica also finds herself trying to figure out the real story behind her mother's relationship with Jake Kane, Lilly's father, who took Lianne to the senior prom when they were both students at Neptune

Veronica Mars and Philosophy: Investigating the Mysteries of Life (Which is a Bitch Until You Die), First Edition. Edited by George A. Dunn.
© 2014 John Wiley & Sons, Inc. Published 2014 by Wiley Blackwell.

High School. Veronica encounters the past and its mysteries everywhere she turns in Neptune; she couldn't escape the power that past events have over her life even if she tried.

On the television screen, *Veronica Mars* presents the past in a unique way, through flashback sequences that employ special visual effects designed to distinguish these sequences from scenes depicting present events. Scenes from the past are always shot in soft focus, with a tint of color that pushes them toward a certain part of the spectrum—blue, green, or orange. These techniques highlight the significance of past events, while portraying them as significantly different from things that take place in the present.

Both the plot and the visual style of *Veronica Mars* assign a huge importance to the past, suggesting that past events have a major impact on the present. But the idea that the past can impact the present is a little bit peculiar. Since events in the past have already happened, we might be inclined to think that they no longer exist, or that they are no longer real. But if the past is no longer real, how can it have an effect on the present? Or does the past have a kind of reality after all, one that can make itself felt in the present?

The French philosopher Gilles Deleuze (1925–1995) argued that the past truly does have reality, though it's a different type of reality from that of the present. Deleuze calls the type of reality belonging to the past "ontological memory" or "the pure past." Through its use of flashbacks and its strong focus on the impact the past has on the present, *Veronica Mars* illustrates Deleuze's theory well and suggests similar ideas about the reality of the past.

"Memories Both Misty and Water-Colored"

The most straightforward way in which the past is accessible to us and has an impact on the present is through everyday memories. Veronica, for example, may wonder what to bake for her friend Wallace Fennel before his big basketball game. Then she remembers that snickerdoodles are his favorite cookie! When we make an effort to remember something, whether a fact or a specific event from the past, we reach into the past and bring it into a relationship with where we stand at this moment. We voluntarily exercise our memory when we recall something on purpose, often in the service of some goal that we're trying to accomplish in the present. We also see this kind of voluntary memory when Veronica discusses with Logan Echolls the Lilly Kane memorial video he's producing by working from material supplied by Lilly's parents, a video that shows her as a young girl riding horses and performing at dance recitals ("The Wrath of Con"). Unconvinced that these images portray Lilly the way she really was, they both recall an episode from the last year's Homecoming Dance, which they think provides a much more accurate picture of Lilly: a girl who loved attention and having a good time. Veronica and Logan voluntarily call up memories of Lilly in order to compare them to what they're currently seeing in the videos of her and conclude that these clips alone wouldn't be a proper tribute to the memory of their friend.

This kind of voluntary remembering is such an everyday occurrence that we rarely stop to think about it or wonder what makes it possible. Certainly Veronica herself doesn't reflect on the metaphysics that underlies her own recollections. Deleuze argues that this power to remember at will can be explained only if we suppose that the past continues to exist in a different type of reality from that of the present. We don't *create* the past through out efforts to remember it, so it must be the case that the past is already all there, though most of it is forgotten. When Deleuze calls this the "pure past," he's referring to the notion that all of the past must exist together, as if recorded on a huge videotape. We gain access to a part of this pure past whenever we make an effort to remember something.

While emphasizing the reality of this pure past, Deleuze also stresses that it exists in a different way from how the present does. Our ability to compare our ordinary voluntary memories with what we see in the present suggests that the past and the present are two different dimensions of time that can be juxtaposed to each other. We often compare what we see in the present to some past memory and ask ourselves whether it's the same thing. For example, the first time Wallace meets Nathan Woods, who claims to be Wallace's father, he can compare Nathan with his memory of the man he's always called his father, Hank Fennel, and he can see that they're definitely not the same person. Deleuze argues that this ability to compare a present experience with a memory, to look for their similarities and differences, proves that the past has a reality separate from the present, which is potentially accessible to our minds. Since we can add a memory to any present experience and then compare the two of them, the past and the present must be different types of experience.

The way *Veronica Mars* depicts past events suggests a similar understanding of the past in its difference from the present. Flashbacks—or any scenes representing past events—are always shot in soft focus and with a colored tint to them, which distinguishes them from scenes belonging to the primary, present-time storyline of the show. This suggests that these scenes, whether they're memories of Lilly or the story of what happened at Shelly Pomeroy's party as recalled by different people ("A Trip to the Dentist"), all belong together as different parts of the pure past. The visual style in which these scenes are presented testifies to the difference between experiencing something as present and remembering it as part of the past.

"I Haven't Thought of You Lately at All"

Much of the time when we voluntarily remember things, it's because something happening now has prompted us to go looking for a memory designed to answer our question. So, for example, when Wallace is working with Veronica to prove that he wasn't the one driving the car that hit a homeless man when he was in Chicago, he searches his memory for people who might have seen him and could corroborate his story. He recalls that, on the night in question, he and his teammate Rashard Rucker were at a fast food drive-through window. The drive-through cashier would certainly remember that Rashard, not Wallace, was driving the car ("Rashard and Wallace Go to White Castle"). In cases like this one, memory and perception are working together compatibly.

Deleuze, however, also calls our attention to a different kind of memory, which doesn't cooperate with our perception of the present—which he calls "reminiscences" or "involuntary memories." An involuntary memory is a "flashback" that's provoked directly by something experienced here and now, without any mental effort to recall something. Deleuze illustrates his notion of involuntary memory by referring to some famous literary examples in the work of the French author Marcel Proust (1871–1922). But several flashbacks on *Veronica Mars* work equally well as examples of this phenomenon. Let's look at a scene from "Credit Where Credit's Due," in which Veronica is on her way to a surfing competition with Duncan and flashes back to a similar scene with her and Lilly, riding in the same car, listening to the same song.

If a specific sound, smell, or taste has ever brought a flood of memories rushing into your mind before you could even consider why, you have an idea of what Deleuze means by an involuntary memory. In the scene we're considering, we don't have the direct access to Veronica's mind that we would need in order to conclude that this flashback is entirely involuntary. However, before the flashback starts, Veronica and Duncan both remark that Lilly loved the song that's playing, which suggests that the song awakened memories of Lilly without any mental effort on the part of Veronica and Duncan. Hearing the song is a sensation that directly triggers another sensation: the reminiscence. Deleuze says that involuntary memory involves a "strict *identity* of a quality common to the two sensations or of a sensation common to the two moments, the present and the past."[1] The song is common to the present and the past moments. But hearing the tune doesn't lead Veronica to search her memories for an answer to the question: "Where have I heard this song before?" Instead, it directly causes the flashback to play in Veronica's mind. It comes to represent all her feelings about the loss of her friend, as if that meaning were packed into the song itself.

This fullness of meaning packed into an involuntary memory distinguishes it from a voluntary recollection. Deleuze insists that what is experienced in an involuntary memory is different from how the event was originally experienced. It is, in a sense, a memory of something that never was present, since the experience, when remembered, means something different from what it did when it actually took place. An episode of involuntary memory captures a truth about the past that one didn't expect to find there. For example, in Veronica's flashback, she and Lilly are talking about how Lilly and Duncan's mother, Celeste Kane, always strongly disapproved of Veronica and Duncan's dating. "Friendly advice? Watch her," says Lilly. "She'll break the two of you up if she can." Given everything that's happened since this conversation took place—Lilly's death, Duncan and Veronica's breakup, and Veronica's suspicion that the Kanes had something to do with Lilly's murder, or at least with covering it up—this conversation takes on an ominous and foreboding character, which it couldn't possibly have had for Veronica at the time.

The meaning expressed in Veronica's flashback doesn't come from comparing it to the present situation that triggered the memory. It brings to mind many things that happened in the past, bolstering her suspicions about the Kanes's involvement in their daughter's death and its cover-up. But at the same time it doesn't give her the whole story—it compels her to keep thinking about what might have happened that night and looking for more clues in order to construct a narrative about Lilly's death and who's responsible for it.

"Even the Experts Agree, a Girl Needs Closure"

The narrative form of detective stories clearly reflects Deleuze's understanding of time; for, on his view, involuntary recollections always present us with significant episodes from the past that push us to think about some problem. From the pilot episode on, flashbacks present parts of a mystery for Veronica, but never the whole truth.

We see the suspicious circumstances surrounding Lilly's murder and the aborted investigation, Duncan's unexplained coldness toward Veronica afterwards, Veronica's mother leaving town and various hints that she may have had some sort of relationship with Jake Kane. Veronica has to try to construct a theory that would explain all these different episodes from the past and fit them together. Did Duncan's mysterious mental illness somehow cause him to kill his sister? Did Veronica's mom leave her dad because she still has romantic feelings for Jake Kane? Does her leaving have any connection to Lilly's murder? Perhaps Abel Koontz agreed to take the fall because he got something from the Kanes in exchange. But what could he have gotten that would be worth going to prison for the rest of his life? When Veronica finds out that Abel Koontz is dying and that Kane Software is making payments to his estranged daughter, a coherent picture starts to emerge. All the while, Veronica can only try to piece the puzzle together, formulate hypotheses that make sense of the available evidence, and look for clues that will support one theory or another.[2]

This process of proposing narratives that draw together different episodes of the past is what Deleuze calls "thought." He argues that an involuntary memory is always like a clue in a mystery, requiring thought in order for us to figure it out. "The echo of the two presents"—the present that we experience now and the present that we remember from the past—"forms only a persistent question, which unfolds within representation like a field of problems, with only the rigorous imperative to search, to respond, to resolve."[3] Episodes from the past always present themselves as parts of a mystery, forcing us to think about how they might fit together coherently.

Deleuze's view of the function of the pure past has much in common with the structure of a detective story. It's as if the past calls out to us, through involuntary memory, to make sense of it, just as the specter of Lilly haunts Duncan, Logan, and Veronica, drawing their attention to things that don't make sense and demanding that they figure them out. On Deleuze's view, our experience in general has the character of a mystery novel. The world is a big, ongoing detective story, calling on us to keep searching for further clues to crack the case.

The final episode of the first season ends with a touching sequence symbolizing the end of one particular detective story. Veronica dreams that she and Lilly are floating together in a pool, surrounded by flower petals, still in the soft focus of the past, but without the dark tints of foreboding and mystery. Veronica asks: "This is how it's going to be from now on, right, Lilly?" Now that the mystery surrounding Lilly's death is solved, Veronica wants her friend back the way it was before her death. But without the pressing mystery to solve, memories of Lilly will no longer force themselves on her, demanding that she crack the case. "Don't forget about me, Veronica," Lilly says before she disappears ("Leave It to Beaver"). Of course Veronica won't forget, but now she'll have to make an effort to remember her friend voluntarily. This can have a melancholy aspect—when you've worked so hard to solve a problem, it can be sad to see it fade away. Luckily, in life as in *Veronica Mars*, there's always another mystery waiting around the next corner.

Notes

1. Gilles Deleuze, *Proust and Signs*, trans. Richard Howard (Minneapolis: University of Minnesota Press, 2004), 59.
2. For more on how Veronica constructs theories and narratives to account for disparate pieces of evidence, see Chapter 14 in this volume, by Daniel A. Wilkenfeld.
3. Gilles Deleuze, *Difference and Repetition*, trans. Paul Patton (New York: Columbia University Press, 1995), 85.

Part III

VERONICA MARS DOESN'T HANG WITH THE EVIL AND MORALLY BANKRUPT

INVESTIGATING VICE AND VIRTUE

"I'm Old School, an Eye for an Eye"
Veronica and Vengeance

George A. Dunn

"Someone's always supposed to pay, right?" Logan Echolls asks Veronica Mars. "Isn't that the rule we live by?"

It's a timely question. Logan has just exacted *payment* from Stosh "Piz" Piznarski in a particularly brutal fashion, battering him bloody for his presumed crime of taping himself and Veronica in a naked romp. Veronica isn't pleased and, frankly, she has no shortage of reasons to be furious at Logan's actions, starting with the fact that "it wasn't Piz, and it could not be less of your business" ("The Bitch Is Back"). But she can't really deny that the "rule" Logan cites has pretty much been her lodestar for the past three years. Veronica Mars is many things—courageous, resourceful, tenacious, witty, and smarter than Don Lamb—but forgiving isn't one of them. She may no longer believe in a Santa Claus, an Easter Bunny, or angels watching over us, but she sure as hell believes in payback.

Veronica Mars and Philosophy: Investigating the Mysteries of Life (Which is a Bitch Until You Die), First Edition. Edited by George A. Dunn.
© 2014 John Wiley & Sons, Inc. Published 2014 by Wiley Blackwell.

"The Bitch Is Back"

The word "revenge" has come to have decidedly negative connotations these days. Psychologists warn that the instinct to retaliate is unhealthy, and they extol the therapeutic benefits of forgiving and forgetting. Holding on to resentment shackles us to the past and impedes our enjoyment of the present, they say. Moralists insist that "two wrongs don't make a right." The Greek philosopher Socrates (469–399 BCE) may have been the first to argue this point, saying: "One must never do wrong in return, nor do any man harm, no matter what he may have done to you."[1] To deliberately seek to harm another person—not as a means to some greater good such as moral improvement, but as an end in itself—is, according to Socrates, intrinsically evil, regardless of who the victim is. Many people would agree that the desire for revenge is a vice, since no truly virtuous person would ever take pleasure in another person's suffering.[2]

Of course, our discomfort with the idea of vengeance doesn't mean that we're opposed to justice. After all, justice and vengeance are leagues apart. Justice remains cool, detached, and objective, even—or especially—with respect to those who've injured us. The just person metes out deserts in an even-handed fashion that isn't clouded by personal feelings. Vengeance, on the other hand, is the quintessential passion of the victim. It's a visceral instinct, not a high-minded aspiration. If our image of justice is a tall, dignified woman, wearing a blindfold and holding a set of scales that represent her devotion to equity and balance, then the essence of vengeance may be well captured in the image of Veronica's classmate Mandy, wild-eyed and screaming as she repeatedly tasers dognapper Hans, whom she has pinned beneath her on the floor of the Neptune dog pound ("Hot Dog").

Still, maybe we're being too hasty in our condemnation of vengeance. After all, it's not for nothing that people say that revenge is sweet. And, as for any qualms about the morality of revenge, it's hard not to sympathize with Mandy's anger as she punishes the creep who she believes has murdered her dog. They say that payback's a bitch. Well, the bitch is back.

Neptune, a Town without Mercy

Veronica isn't the only person in Neptune who lives by the rule of payback. In fact, a significant number of her cases involve uncovering what turns out to be elaborate and often highly ingenious schemes to get revenge. Pete Kaminski builds a web site implicating the former bully Norton Clayton in a bomb threat against the school, thereby exacting revenge for years of bullying that culminated in a beating that put Pete in the hospital and turned his father against him ("Weapons of Class Destruction"). Gay Neptune student Ryan torments the bereaved parents of Marcos Oliveres, whom Ryan blames for shipping Marcos off to a "deprogramming" camp for gays and for indirectly causing his death ("Ahoy Mateys"). The women of Lilith House take revenge on Chip Diller, whose cruel mockery of Patrice Petrelli caused her to have an emotional breakdown and to stroll off the roof of the Theta Beta House to escape further ridicule. The Lilith House women kidnap him, shave his head, and rape him with a "keister egg" ("Lord of the Pi's"). And Carrie Bishop seeks revenge against Neptune High teacher Chuck Rooks, destroying his reputation by falsely accusing him of getting her pregnant and then callously tossing money at her to "take care of it" ("Mars vs. Mars").

In an interesting twist, however, it turns out that Carrie is pursuing revenge not on her own behalf, but for her friend Susan Knight, who really *did* become pregnant by Mr. Rooks and then dropped out of school to have the baby after declining the $500 he offered her to pay for the abortion. "It made her crazy there were no consequences for what he did," Susan tells Veronica, explaining Carrie's actions. Carrie is a high-status 09-er, who, according to Veronica, has enjoyed "a long and storied reign as the gossip queen of Neptune High" ("Mars vs. Mars"). Given what Carrie's revenge scheme costs her in public disgrace, we'd have to describe her action as both altruistic and self-sacrificial, in addition to being an act of spite.

Logan is also willing to endure a cost in order to make others pay. Upon learning that Mercer Hayes had attacked Veronica, Logan smashes the windshield of a sheriff's department vehicle just so he can be arrested and placed in the same cell with Mercer, whereupon Logan proceeds to mete out his own brand of justice with his fists ("Spit & Eggs"). Maybe adding one more arrest to his ever-growing criminal record isn't that great a sacrifice for Logan—he's already been arrested twice for murder—but one of his later acts of vengeance borders on the suicidal. In the Hearst College cafeteria, Logan delivers a very public smackdown of Goryan "Gory" Sorokin, the sleazebag responsible for distributing the Veronica-Piz sex tape. Veronica backs off seeking revenge against Gory once she learns of his family's Mafia connections, and she warns Logan to do the same. When Gory tells Logan, "Whoever you are, you're gonna die," we have every reason to believe that he means business, so the cost of that act of vengeance could conceivably be *very* high ("The Bitch Is Back").

Carrie Bishop is willing to destroy her own reputation in order to get revenge against Mr. Rooks. Logan doesn't mind making himself the target of a Mafia hit, as long as this means that Gory Sorokin pays a price for what he did to Veronica. And Veronica will torpedo her shot at the Kane Scholarship, along with her chance to go to Stanford, in order to be in court and enjoy the vindictive pleasure of watching the expression on Aaron Echolls's face when the jury foreman finds him guilty. "I wanna see that smirk wiped from his face," she says. "I wanna see his expression at the exact moment he realizes he'll never be a free man again" ("Happy Go Lucky"). The pleasure that she anticipates is more than simple satisfaction at justice being done.

It's personal. Justice may objectively decree that Aaron spend the rest of his life behind bars, but Veronica's willingness to sacrifice Stanford—her dream since elementary school—just to witness his agony and despair bespeaks her desire for vengeance. As it turns out, Aaron left the courtroom a free man, with his smirk more deeply etched into his face than ever, so Veronica lost her scholarship for nothing. And she wasn't even there to witness how justice caught up with Aaron the next night at the Neptune Grand, when Clarence Weidman, acting on behalf of Duncan Kane, put a bullet in the back of the skull of the man who murdered Duncan's sister ("Not Pictured").

A taste for vengeance can be costly, so much so that we might wonder whether it's really worth it. Is the desire for vengeance rational? Even if pursuing revenge doesn't require you to forfeit a scholarship, trash your reputation, or imperil your life, it may still entail an enormous expenditure of time and effort—and for what? When Veronica offers Carmen Ruiz the opportunity to strike back at Tad Wilson after he shares a video of her that's intended to make her a laughingstock, she declines, explaining: "Tearing Tad down isn't gonna make me feel any better" ("M.A.D."). Maybe we feel proud of Carmen for proving that she's better than Tad, but her inability to derive personal gratification from an act of revenge puts her in a distinct, if saintly, minority.

"Shut Up, Sane Veronica—I'm in Charge Now!"

Rational or not, it's a fact of human nature that people are often willing to incur costs in order to make other people "pay" for their transgressions. Consider an experiment devised by game theorists, known as "the ultimatum game."[3] It works something like this. Suppose that someone offers morally bankrupt Neptune private investigator Vincent Van Lowe twenty shares of stock in Kane Software, free of charge, but on condition that he share some of his windfall with local legal beagle Cliff McCormack, who happens to be standing at his side. What's more, Vinnie must declare in advance how much he plans to give to Cliff, who can either accept or reject the proposed division. However, if Cliff declines, they both get nothing. According to the standard model of economic rationality, not to mention Vinnie's standard modus vivendi of unabashed greed, the sensible thing would be for him to give Cliff as little as possible, no more than a single share. And the sensible thing would be for Cliff to accept it, since a single share is better than nothing.

But that's not how the ultimatum game usually plays out in the laboratory. For starters, real-world researchers typically offer the players cold hard cash rather than shares of Kane Stock. More importantly, if one player proposes a division that strikes the other as too greedy, the one who feels slighted will most often refuse the offer and both will get nothing. This looks like a classic case of "cutting off your nose to spite your face," that is, engaging in an act of vengeance even though you know that you'll end up hurting yourself in the process. But that's precisely what most people do. If revenge is irrational, then it seems that most of us, at least sometimes, relish wrath over reason. The need to settle scores is a passion that seems to run as deep in human nature as the desire for sex or hunger, though it may be less immediately clear what good it serves.

If the desire for revenge is often irrational, it crosses the line into something close to total insanity for Veronica in "There's Got to Be a Morning after Pill." Of course, this is only because a perfect storm of emotionally fraught elements—her distrust of Logan, her bitter memories of the events and aftermath of Shelly Pomeroy's party, and (gasoline on the fire) the return of the loathsome Madison Sinclair—has come together to keep Veronica sleep-deprived and obsessed with punishing the stuck-up 09-er. If Carrie Bishop was made "crazy" by the absence of consequences for Mr. Rooks, Veronica is completely unhinged by the fresh insult that Madison has added to the injury she inflicted at Shelly's party, when her "trip to the dentist" resulted in Veronica's being raped: it turns out that over the winter break Madison slept with Logan. Veronica breaks up with Logan, but that's not enough to get the image of him with Madison out of her head. This is an affront that won't stay buried in the past, where it belongs, but returns again and again, to haunt Veronica's dreams and to overrun her imagination every time she spies a blonde of Madison's build. Many of us have probably had a similar experience of suffering some profound indignity or betrayal that just keeps barging its way back into our consciousness against our will, incessantly reopening the wound and refreshing the pain. Her torment is something to which many of us can relate.

Veronica's experience in this episode can give us some insight into what it is that the vengeful person actually *gets* from her act of vengeance that could be worth the price tag that it often carries. Veronica begins stalking Madison because, as Veronica explains in a voiceover (or is this just her mumbling to herself deliriously?): "When I'm lying in bed and I can't sleep because of visions of Madison and Logan rolling around, she wins. When I got her in my sights, I'm in control." The key word here is "control." As long as Madison has a free run of Veronica's imagination, Veronica still feels like a victim, at the mercy of someone she despises. One of the worst aspects of being a victim—perhaps in some ways worse than more tangible damages, like physical injury or loss of property—is the feeling of powerlessness, in particular, of being unable to demand the respect that we feel we are due. And, in Veronica's case, the sting of Madison's disrespect simply won't go away, compounding the sense of powerlessness.

This feeling of being at the mercy of another can strike a terrible blow to our pride—or to what people nowadays often call our "self-esteem." Psychologist Roy Baumeister describes the relationship between revenge and wounded self-esteem as follows:

What prompts people to take strong measures to get revenge? The main answer appears to be threats to their self-esteem. … Being humiliated, embarrassed, treated with disrespect, made a fool of, or otherwise attacked on this dimension of worthiness is an important cause of violence, because it creates strong urges to take revenge.[4]

When the avenger seeks to make someone "pay" for an affront, damaged self-esteem or diminished status is the loss for which compensation is demanded and pain is the only coin that will be accepted as payment. The philosopher Friedrich Nietzsche (1844–1900) also associated the execution of revenge with the recovery of a loss of self-esteem and status:

Through his "punishment" of the debtor the creditor participates in a *right of lords*: finally he, too, for once attains the elevated feeling of being permitted to hold a being in contempt and maltreat it as something "beneath himself"…[5]

Vengeance turns grief into grievance. Grief—the pain and humiliation of having been abused—is demoralizing and debilitating. But to act out a grievance can be empowering. Whereas grief is suffered passively, a grievance can give you an active purpose. You can do things with grievance, like pay Eli "Weevil" Navarro $500 to steal Madison's new Mercedes, with its personalized "GOTZMINE" license plate, and to crush it into the shape of a cube.

Oh, How the Mighty Have Softened!

In "There's Got to Be a Morning after Pill," Veronica meets her polar opposite (at least when it comes to revenge) in the reverend Ted Capistrano, a cable-access televangelist and pastor of Capistrano Ministries. The reverend's daughter Bonnie had hired Veronica to uncover who it was that slipped Bonnie a dose of RU-486 that caused her to have a miscarriage. When the culprit turns out to be her roommate and lifelong friend Phyllis, who didn't want Bonnie to sacrifice her career plans for the shackles of motherhood, she can barely control her fury. "Go to hell! Go to hell!" she screams. Like most evangelical Christians, Reverend Ted is a firm believer in the sanctity of life from the moment of conception and, though we don't know all the details of his theology, his religion has traditionally taught that hell is just where an unrepentant sinner deserves to go. So we might expect him to endorse his daughter's words, as well as the punitive impulse behind them. But the reverend surprises us by embracing Bonnie as she trembles in rage and by urging her to practice forgiveness:

> She didn't mean to hurt you. Try to be forgiving. It's the only way. Anger will tear you down. It'll make you less of the person that you want to be. Anger will tear apart your soul. The Bible teaches us that he who is slow to anger is better than the mighty and he who rules his spirit than he who captures the city. He who is slow to anger has great understanding, but he who is quick tempered exalts folly.[6]

One might reasonably wonder whether lecturing his daughter on the virtue of forgiveness and the immorality of anger is really the most compassionate response available to the reverend at the moment. After all, most of us would agree that Bonnie has every right to be furious. So, if hurling a few curses Phyllis's way helps Bonnie reclaim a little bit of the agency that's been stolen from her, then what's the harm? Regardless of whether Reverend Ted's general point is sound, it seems almost cruel for him to censure his daughter's perfectly understandable anger after she's been the victim of such a massive betrayal by a trusted friend. But let's try to forgive the reverend's lapse in pastoral sensitivity long enough to consider whether he in fact might have a point.

Does anger, the sort that aims at harming the other person in retaliation, really diminish the angry person?

The Book of Proverbs, the Old Testament "wisdom" book from which Reverend Ted quotes, associates being slow to anger with strength, self-control, and understanding. By implication, the passion for vengeance signifies weakness, self-indulgence, and folly. Most interestingly, the person who's slow to anger is compared to a warrior who conquers a city, which is somewhat surprising, since the exploits of one of the greatest warriors of antiquity are recorded in a book (the *Iliad*) that opens with a reference to rage. But it's not the fury of the warrior that the Book of Proverbs highlights, but rather his ability to conquer. And, although the poets of antiquity—including the poets of the Old Testament—never cease to sing the praises of those rare heroes who have the strength, will, and discipline needed to capture a city and subdue its inhabitants, the Book of Proverbs suggests that even greater praise is due to the unsung hero in ordinary life who is able to subdue his anger. Veronica's last name is Mars, same as the Roman god of war. The suggestion here is that all that martial energy she directs against her enemies could more nobly be deployed to hold in check her own appetite for vengeance.

This biblical teaching on anger reflects a view that's shared by many of the greatest Western philosophers, including Plato (427–347 BCE), who proposed in the *Republic* and in the *Timaeus* that *thumos* or "spirit"—the energy of the soul that finds expression in pride and anger—be directed to quelling the unruly passions and bringing them under the rule of reason. The Roman philosopher Seneca (4 BCE–65 CE) called anger "the most hideous and frenzied of all emotions" and claimed that "men possessed by anger are insane," a description that certainly fits Veronica in the throes of her Madison-induced madness.[7] And, although the virtuous person would vigorously fight for justice and defend the innocent, Seneca believed that she would do so out of a sense of duty alone rather than out of anger or an appetite for revenge. Seneca would find nothing to commend in Veronica's desire to watch Aaron's smirk evaporate as the verdict was read, let alone in her desire to crush and cube Madison's car. Seneca, Plato, and Proverbs are all in agreement: to act from anger is not at all empowering. On the contrary, it's to relinquish the reigns of the soul to what is most base and petty within it.

We don't know how persuasive Bonnie ultimately found her father's off-the-cuff sermon on forgiveness, but it seems to have had an effect on Veronica. With Reverend Ted's words still ringing in her ears—and apparently drowning out the Madison tape that's been in heavy mental rotation for most of the episode—Veronica arrives at the scrap yard to let Weevil know that she's had a change of heart and would like to cancel her "crush and cube" order. "Maybe you could open a can of tuna, put it insider her A/C vent, then park it back on the block," she suggests when Weevil seems disappointed. "You're going soft, Mars," he says.

"Do You Not Instinctively Fear Me?"

Wait! We don't want to see Veronica go soft! Must Reverend Ted have the last word? Is there anything positive left to be said on behalf of revenge? Sure, it can be costly (though $500 to crush and cube Madison's Mercedes doesn't sound altogether unreasonable) and, sure, it may not have the most wholesome effects on your soul (its recuperative effect on damaged self-esteem notwithstanding). But might revenge have other benefits, which could make the "rule" of retaliation a rational one to follow? There's at least one.

The great political philosopher Niccolò Machiavelli (1469–1527) once posed the question of whether it is better for an ambitious person to be feared or loved. Both love and fear can elicit the cooperation of others, so the ideal would be to somehow combine the advantages of both. But he concluded in the end that, "because it is difficult to put them together, it is much safer to be feared than loved, if one has to lack one of the two."[8] He based his conclusion on the fact that most people are "ungrateful" and "fickle," their affections liable to melt away when the going gets tough or sometimes for no discernible reason at all. If you're counting on people's love to ensure good treatment for you, you may be in for an unpleasant surprise, as Meg Manning discovers when she becomes the victim of a false "purity test" score. The envious Meg-wanna-be Kimmy had posted the score for the sole purpose of destroying Meg's reputation. Suddenly Meg finds herself shunned and "slut-sneezed" in the halls of Neptune High by her former friends among the 09-ers. But, once Veronica exposes the fraud, Meg is welcomed back into the fickle embrace of the same classmates who spurned her.[9]

"All of a sudden everyone's running up to me saying how they never believed I did those things," Meg reports to Veronica with a happy bounce in her step.

VERONICA   Funny. No one's come running up to me.
MEG   It's because people are afraid of you.
VERONICA   Then something's working. ("Like a Virgin")

Veronica learned her own lesson about fickleness and ingratitude the year before, when her father's pursuit of Jake Kane for the Lilly Kane murder lost Veronica her access to the social world beyond the "velvet ropes" ("Pilot"). Unlike Meg, Veronica can't assume that her default status is one that commands the respect she's due. As she tells her bullied classmate Mandy: "If you want people to leave you alone, Mandy, or, better yet, treat you with respect, demand it. Make them." But the only way you can credibly make such a demand is to sell everyone on the idea that you're prepared to bring hell and misery crashing down around their ears if they don't respect you. "If you use Mandy again to try to convince yourself that you're not a loser, I will ruin your life," Veronica informs Lenny Sofer, who has been tormenting Mandy since he discovered last year that she had a crush on him ("Hot Dogs"). Veronica can do it too. I would wager Piz's 1967 Gretsch Astro-jet Red-Top guitar that Lenny starts showing Mandy some respect from now on.

And how much do you want to bet that it will be a long, long time before poor tasered Hans considers stealing another dog?

Notes

1. Plato, Crito, 49c; in G. M. A. Grube, ed. and trans., *The Trial and Death of Socrates* (3rd edn., Indianapolis, IN: Hackett, 2000), 50.
2. The term for taking pleasure in the suffering of another person is *Schadenfreude*, which contemporary philosopher Colin McGinn insists is always evil. See his *Evil, Ethics, and Fiction* (New York: Oxford University Press, 1997), 61.
3. Matt Ridley discusses the ultimatum game in his book *The Origins of Virtue: Human Instincts and the Evolution of Cooperation* (New York: Penguin Books, 2004), 139–140.
4. Roy F. Baumeister, *Evil: Inside Human Violence and Cruelty* (New York: W. H. Freeman, 2000), 152.
5. Friedrich Nietzsche, *On the Genealogy of Morality*, trans. Maudemarie Clark and Alan J. Swensen (Indianapolis, IN: Hackett, 1998), 41.
6. The Reverend Ted is quoting Proverbs 16: 32 and 14: 29 (New American Standard Bible).
7. Lucius Annaeus Seneca, *Moral and Political Essays*, ed. and trans. J. M. Cooper and J. F. Procopé (Cambridge: Cambridge University Press, 1995), 17.
8. Niccolò Machiavelli, *The Prince*, trans. Harvey C. Mansfield (2nd edn., Chicago: University of Chicago Press, 1998), 66.
9. For more on the "purity test" and its relationship to sexual objectification, see Chapter 12 in this volume, by Jordan Pascoe.

8

"We Used to be Friends"
An Aristotelian Analysis of Veronica's Friendships

Catlyn Origitano

The girls' bathroom at Neptune High serves as Veronica Mars's informal office space for much of the first two seasons of the show. Veronica's fellow Pirates know that she will be there to take on the case of anyone who can pay—09-er, PCH-er, nerd, and jock alike. In a familiar scene, Veronica is approached by one such peer and asked to do some detective work. She informs him that she does "favors for friends." After he tells her that he can pay, Veronica answers: "Sit down, friend" ("Silence of the Lamb").

This interaction between Veronica and a client, facetiously called "friend," raises questions about what a friend really is and how we can know when we've found a real friend. The Greek philosopher Aristotle (384–322 BCE) thought a lot about these questions a long time ago, but what he said still applies to the *noir* world of Neptune today.

"I Do Favors for Friends"

Aristotle looks at friendship in his classic work *Nicomachean Ethics*, which examines the question: "What is a good life for a human being?" If we want good lives, according to Aristotle,

Veronica Mars and Philosophy: Investigating the Mysteries of Life (Which is a Bitch Until You Die), First Edition. Edited by George A. Dunn.
© 2014 John Wiley & Sons, Inc. Published 2014 by Wiley Blackwell.

friendship is indispensible, not just because we need friends to perform various favors for us but because friendship is in itself a "noble" thing, something praiseworthy and desirable for its own sake. But not all friendships are equal. Aristotle identifies three forms of friendship. What they have in common is that they're all based on love or affection for another person, but they differ according to what it is that we find lovable about that person.[1]

The first form of friendship is friendship of utility, in which the friends value each other primarily for various benefits they get out of the relationship.[2] Keith Mars's relationship with attorney Cliff McCormack falls into this category. We don't see them hanging out together just for fun, but they seem to be on very good terms and each likes the other enough to send business his way. The mutual benefit they derive from their relationship seems to be what keeps their friendship going. But suppose Cliff decided to get out of the law business and could no longer refer clients to Keith. It's doubtful that the two of them would continue to have much of a relationship, since it's only mutual benefit or utility that sustains their friendship in the first place.

A "friendship" of utility may seem to be stretching the meaning of the word a bit. What Keith and Cliff have going is something we might be more inclined to call a "professional partnership," or maybe a successful case of "networking," distinguishing it from the sort of relationship where we enjoy the other person's company for its own sake, not just as a means to an end. But it's clear that Keith and Cliff do in fact like each other. There's a warmth to their interactions that makes them more than just impersonal business transactions. Aristotle would certainly call them friends.

Aristotle's second form of friendship, however, probably fits more closely with the way many of us use that word today. In what Aristotle calls a friendship of pleasure, the friends associate with each because they derive genuine pleasure from being in each other's company and from the activities they share.[3] Logan Echolls and Dick Casablancas enjoy the time they spend together doing fun things like surfing, partying, and setting fire to the community pool at the city park ("Normal Is the Watchword"). Those pleasurable activities are what cements the bond between the two of them. As long as they continue to share the same interests and enjoy each other's antics, they are likely to remain friends. However, we see them growing apart somewhat during their first year at Hearst College. There are a number of factors that account for the increasing distance in their relationship, but it probably has at least something to do with the fact that they're both maturing somewhat—though clearly not at the same rate—and coming to have different interests and values that they may not necessarily share. Aristotle notes that this is not an uncommon development in friendships of pleasure, since this sort of friendship is most common among young people and, as we're constantly reminded by all the drama in the halls of Neptune High and Hearst College, young people tend to base their decisions on their often mercurial emotions. The friendship of pleasure lasts as long as everyone is having fun, but once the "fun, fun, fun" has run its course ("Pilot"), so too will the friendship. And this is what leads Aristotle to conclude that, in a friendship based merely on pleasure, one doesn't love the friend for his own sake, but rather for the pleasure one derives from his company.

Friendships of utility and friendships of pleasure can combine in various ways. The friendship between Logan and Dick is primarily about sharing good times, but the two do each other plenty of favors as well. Dick shows up crying on Logan's doorstep when he "doesn't have anywhere else to go" and is welcomed and comforted, though no one is having much fun at the moment ("Welcome Wagon"). And Dick comes to Logan's assistance as well. Dick is part of the 09-er posse that Logan rounds up to go after Chardo Navarro, who had been carrying on with Logan's girlfriend Caitlin Ford behind his back ("Credit Where Credit's Due"). Similarly, though the friendship between Keith and Cliff seems to be based primarily on utility, the clever repartee that they regularly exchange makes it clear that they also find each other's company pleasant. And then there are those mildly scandalous hybrid relationships, such as the trophy marriage of Kendall and Richard "Big Dick" Casablancas, where one person is seeking pleasure while the other has her eye on a different sort of benefit. This example highlights another point about friendships for pleasure: they include romantic relationships, and even relationships where the pleasure sought is purely erotic, as when Logan and Kendall become "buddies."

"Mom Seems to Like Him"

Though most friendships, including most friendships in Neptune, fall into one or both of these two categories, Aristotle believes that there's something incomplete or imperfect about them. Though we may feel affection for those who give us pleasure and provide us with benefits, what we really love in those friendships, he argues, is the things we get out of the relationship: the fun and the profit. But, in the perfect form of friendship, what sustains the relationship is something much deeper, namely the two friends' love and admiration for each other, which is based on a recognition of the other's goodness, excellence, or virtuous moral character.[4] This perfect form of friendship can exist only between good people who are alike in virtue. And, since moral character is more enduring than either pleasure or utility, this form of friendship lasts longer and is harder to dissolve than the two other inferior and imperfect forms.

People sometimes say that they want to be loved for themselves, not just for their looks or their money. Aristotle would say that what they want is this third, perfect form of friendship, a friendship of virtue. Aristotle calls this form of friendship "perfect" or "complete" not just because it's focused on the intrinsic qualities of the friend herself, but also because it includes the other two. After all, having good people as friends is both useful and pleasant. Whom on *Veronica Mars* could we offer as an example of this perfectly virtuous friend? Wallace Fennel's friend Norman, of course!

VERONICA Who's Norman?

WALLACE Norman is my imaginary, straight A, Eagle Scout, mama's boy friend.

VERONICA He sounds boring for an imaginary friend.

WALLACE Mom seems to like him.

What makes Norman so appealing to Alicia Fennel is that he fulfills one of the most important functions that Aristotle assigns to a good and virtuous friend: he models the right sort of behavior, holding both himself and his friends to high standards. Norman upholds the right moral "norms" and, to the extent that we care about virtue ourselves, we can't help but admire him, even apart from any benefits we receive from him. But being friends with Norman *would* most likely be both beneficial and pleasurable for anyone as fully committed to the same "straight A, Eagle Scout" levels of excellence. He's the best friend a mom could want for her boy.

The only drawback to Norman is that he's non-existent. And the only drawback to this highest form of friendship is that it sometimes comes close to being non-existent as well. Aristotle, at least, acknowledges that it's very rare.[5] It's so rare in fact that Veronica may have never found herself in such a friendship. But perhaps we shouldn't be surprised that friendships based on virtue are so rare in a town where virtue itself is in such short supply. Let's look at some of the most important friendships Veronica has formed over the course of the series and consider the extent to which they approach or fall short of Aristotelian perfection.

"How about You Do Me a Favor for Once?"

When we first meet Wallace, he's a new student at Neptune High. From the start, his relationship with Veronica exemplifies Aristotle's friendship of utility. Their relationship begins on the first day of school, when Veronica removes a duct-taped Wallace from the school flagpole. Veronica subsequently helps Wallace by retrieving from the sheriff department's evidence locker a video taken at the Sac N Pac where Wallace works, which shows a pair of PCH-ers shoplifting ("Pilot"). At this early stage, Veronica and Wallace are not yet friends in Aristotle's sense, since every form of friendship, including one of utility, needs some time to get off the ground. As Aristotle explains, "one cannot extend friendship or be a friend of another person until each partner has impressed the other that he is worthy of affection."[6] But, even if they're not friends just yet, we see the groundwork for their friendship laid as Veronica shows Wallace just how helpful—and hence "worthy of affection"—she can be.

Wallace soon has the opportunity to show Veronica just how worthy of affection he is too. Leaving the school office, Veronica bumps into Wallace on his way in. She's surprised, yet pleased, to learn that he'll be working there this semester as an office aide. "That's great!" she exclaims. "For me." She then presents Wallace with the first of many assignments to come: "I need you to copy all of Weevil's attendance records from this past month and get them to me" ("Credit Where Credit Is Due"). What's beginning to emerge here is reciprocal utility, where each party has impressed its usefulness on the other. From such ground, a friendship of utility can begin to blossom.

This pattern of Veronica and Wallace being useful to each other continues throughout the first season. Wallace seeks Veronica's help in recovering the money a couple of computer nerds had swindled from his would-be girlfriend Georgia, an object of his affection, on whom he wants to impress his own "worthiness." "I'm hungry for gratitude," he tells Veronica. She, in turn, uses

Wallace as an escort to a college party, where she investigates the nerds' criminal doings ("The Wrath of Con"). Later in the season, as Wallace munches down a snickerdoodle that she had just baked for him, she inquires: "Can you do me a weird favor without asking any questions?" "Isn't that the bedrock upon which our friendship was founded?" he responds, explicitly describing their relationship as one founded on the solid rock of utility ("Betty and Veronica").

While friendships of utility thrive on an exchange of goods between friends, Aristotle argues that these friendships can dissolve into acrimony and resentment if one friend feels that she's giving more than she gets in return.[7] That's why complaints often arise in friendships of utility, including the friendship between Wallace and Veronica. Tensions in their relationship come to a head around the time Wallace finds out that his biological father is *not* Hank Fennell, as he had always believed, but rather a shady character named Nathan Woods, who suddenly appears outside his house one day. To add even more drama to the mix, Jackie Cook, Wallace's girlfriend, had just played a malicious prank on Veronica by getting the fake "psychic," Madam Sophie, to announce on her show that Veronica had used the breast enhancement cream Mamma-Max—an embarrassing secret, which Veronica had recently confided in Jackie. Not being one to let things like these slide, Veronica has already worked out her plan for revenge, but Wallace pleads with her to "let it go" this time. "How about you do me a favor for once?" he asks. "Why does it have to be about you all of the time?"

He then proceeds to remind her of how little she's been giving recently in this relationship, which is supposedly based on give-and-take:

> Have you been payin' any attention lately? I just learned my whole life is a lie. My dad isn't my dad. I've always been a shoulder you can lean on. You've given me no time, no sympathy, nothing. ("Blast from the Past")

Veronica is at an unusual loss for words after this well-deserved scolding. She has a change of heart and abandons her revenge plan, in effect acknowledging the justice of Wallace's complaint that their relationship had become unfairly one-sided and that it's high time for her to start returning the favors he's done for her. It's a good thing she gets the message, too, for otherwise their friendship would very likely have soon been over. Such complaints of unequal reciprocity are all too common in friendships of utility, according to Aristotle, and they are the reason why these friendships often end ugly.

Not all of Veronica's relationships are based primarily on utility, however. Like most young people, she also forms friendships of pleasure. And, of all her relationships, the one that seems to have given the greatest pleasure to fans is her rollercoaster romance with Logan, the dreamy bad boy with a wit as sharp as hers. Logan occupies a unique position in Veronica's life, as he changes from friend to enemy to ally to lover and then back to just friends again, over the course of three seasons.

What keeps drawing them to each other? There's no mistaking their irrepressible sexual chemistry—even when Veronica claimed to hate Logan, she still couldn't seem to keep her lips off him ("Weapons of Class Destruction")—but perhaps equally important is the pleasure they take in each other's wit, something Aristotle himself highlights as contributing to the durability of a friendship of pleasure.[8] Both Veronica and Logan are known for their quick one-liners and snappy comebacks, which they regularly unleash on each other. Perhaps it's the shared sense of humor that makes him a more appealing partner for Veronica than her other love interests, Duncan Kane and Stosh "Piz" Piznarski— sweet guys who lack that razor-sharp wit.

Of course, Veronica's relationship with Logan isn't *merely* a friendship of pleasure. After all, the two begin their friendship in mutual use: Logan enlists Veronica to help him find answers regarding his mother's death ("Mars vs. Mars") and later brings his fists to Veronica's rescue when he thinks she's in danger from undercover Bureau of Alcohol, Tobacco, and Firearms agent Ben ("Weapons of Class Destruction"). By the same token, Veronica's friendship with Wallace isn't only about utility. They enjoy each other's company, so they clearly enjoy a friendship of pleasure as well. Veronica bakes cookies for Wallace and secretly puts them in his locker, which shows us that she's genuinely interested in his happiness and not simply investing in him as a future benefactor ("Betty and Veronica"). Still, neither of these relationships rises to the level of Aristotle's highest form of friendship: a perfect friendship based on virtue. And, although we don't have the space to look at every friendship Veronica forms over the course of the series, it's probably safe to say that, if these two key friendships fall short, her others will as well.

"I'm Not Built That Way"

Aristotle argues that, in order to have a perfect friendship, both friends must be good and virtuous people; so let's investigate the moral characters of these two close friends to see if either can be considered truly virtuous.[9] Wallace is an admirable person in many respects, but his moral character is still wanting. His entrance into Veronica's life is due to his witnessing a crime about which he lied to the cops in order to save his own skin ("Pilot"). He cheats on his present girlfriend, Jane Kuhne, with his former girlfriend, Jackie ("Plan B"); and he leaves his friends and family without saying a word ("Blast from the Past"), returning only to avoid a serious problem in Chicago that, once again, involves his covering for someone who had committed a crime. To his credit, though, this time he feels remorse for taking the coward's way out. "You'd have done the right thing," he tells Veronica. "I'm embarrassed I didn't" ("Donut Run"). Wallace makes another bad decision as a student at Hearst College: he cheats on a test because he's struggling with the class ("President Evil"). After he's caught, though, he seems to change his ways.

He studies for class, accepts responsibility for his actions, and moves forward. And at the end of his freshman year he signs up as a volunteer to travel to Uganda with Invisible Children, an organization working to protect youths in that war-ravaged country ("I Know What You'll Do Next Summer"). Wallace appears to be on the track to virtue; but, during his years at Neptune and his first year at Hearst, he's clearly not there yet.

Logan doesn't make the virtuous cut either. He supplied the gamma-hydroxybutyric acid (GHB) that ultimately led to Veronica's rape ("M.A.D."); he organized bum fights ("Return of the Kane"); and he fled from a fire that Mercer Hayes had started in a Tijuana hotel room instead of sticking around to help ("Of Vice and Men"). And there's more, much more, but we only have so much space. Some may want to argue that Logan matured and had become a better person by the time the show ended. And indeed he seems to have turned a corner. He started treating Veronica better, attended his classes, and cared for his friend Dick. But, as with Wallace, we get to see only the beginning of what will undoubtedly be a long journey for Logan. And, despite his movement toward becoming a better person, Logan—the "obligatory psychotic jackass" of Neptune High— still has a long way to go before we can call him a truly virtuous person ("Pilot").

And then there's Veronica herself. How virtuous is she? There are so many factors to consider, but let's just focus on one facet of her personality: her lack of trust and trustworthiness. Even Keith, who loves his daughter beyond measure, confesses that he doesn't know how he will ever trust her again after the way she played him in her elaborate ploy to help Duncan and his infant daughter sneak out of the country ("Donut Run"). And being untrustworthy is a significant impediment to friendship, at least according to Aristotle. For him, mutual trust—specifically, the assurance that neither friend will ever wrong the other—is an indispensable requirement for achieving any friendship of serious depth.[10] Aristotle's focus on trust also helps to explain why he believed that true friends must be virtuous. Only virtuous friends can trust each other without fear of betrayal, because only virtuous people are entirely worthy of trust. If, when the going gets tough, Wallace and Logan flee from their troubles—be these a hit-and-run in Chicago or a hotel fire in Tijuana—how can we be sure that, in a moment of weakness, they might not go as far as to betray a friend? For Aristotle, a lack of virtue not only makes someone less lovable. It also makes that person less trustworthy, and this, in turn, makes the same person less choiceworthy as a friend.[11]

The bottom line is that Veronica and her friends ultimately can't trust each other; therefore, they can't enjoy perfect friendships with each other. This is particularly glaring in her romantic relationships. Duncan hides the fact that he suffers from a form of epilepsy that causes him to have violent outbursts. Veronica uncovers his secret only by prying into his medical records, which understandably infuriates him ("Weapons of Class Destruction"). Yet she doesn't seem to be at all remorseful about her snooping. Trust is equally absent from her relationship with Logan, as she openly concedes. When Logan asks her if she trusts him, she responds: "No, I can't. I'm not built that way" ("Of Vice and Men"). Aristotle would shake his head sadly and say that Veronica must therefore not be built to enjoy the perfect form of friendship, which depends on trust and virtue.

"See, This Dame Walks In"

Should we chalk up this failure to achieve perfect friendship to Veronica's own peculiar failings? Or could it rather be a symptom of living in Neptune, a town riddled with murder, theft, betrayal, and intrigue? This atmosphere of corruption is what makes the show so intriguing, and it's what keeps Mars Investigations afloat. But it doesn't seem to have a healthy effect on relationships, Veronica's in particular. Could her world ever be a place where she finds true friendship? *Veronica Mars* belongs to the *film noir* genre, in which the central protagonist is typically disillusioned, cynical, and alienated from society—a description that fits Veronica to a T.[12] After all, this is the girl who tells us in the pilot episode: "If there's something I've learned in this business, the people you love let you down." Veronica inhabits a world of moral ambiguity and double crosses. It's not our world, and certainly not the world of Aristotle. Perhaps in the end it's the *noir* nature of Veronica's world that stands in the way of her having perfect friendships.

However, in the trailer for the *Veronica Mars* movie, we see our protagonist exhibit a level of self-awareness that perhaps wasn't present before. Asked in an interview what her background "says about a person," she responds: "Compulsive, clearly. Addictive personality. Possible adrenaline junky."[13] Veronica seems to realize that outside of Neptune her circumstances and behavior appear abnormal—and that's putting it mildly! Having left her previous occupation behind, she's no longer in the business that taught her that everyone lets you down. Having lived for several years outside the *noir* world of Neptune, maybe she's finally ready to embody the show's theme song in a new way: a long time ago we used to be friends of utility or pleasure, but now I'm ready for a perfect friendship of virtue.

Notes

1. Aristotle, *Nicomachean Ethics*, trans. Martin Ostwald (Upper Saddle River: Prentice Hall, 1999), 215 (1155^{b}16).
2. Ibid., 218 (1156^{a}10–11).
3. Ibid., 218 (1156^{a}15).
4. Ibid., 219 (1156^{b}6–7).
5. Ibid., 220 (1156^{b}25).
6. Ibid., 220 (1156^{b}28–30).

7. Ibid., 240 (1162^{b}5–6).
8. Ibid., 222 (1157^{a}3–5).
9. Ibid., 219 (1156^{b}6–7).
10. Ibid., 222 (1157^{a}23–26).
11. For more on Veronica's difficulty with trust, see Chapter 5, by Daniel Wack, and Chapter 9, by Jon Robson, in this volume.
12. For more on the *film noir* genre, see Chapter 5, by Daniel Wack, and Chapter 6, by James B. South, in this volume.
13. "First Look: The Official Veronica Mars SDCC Sneak Peak," http://www.youtube.com/watch?v=LVJhjV3EOY4 (accessed July 26, 2013).

9

Does Veronica Trust Anyone?

Jon Robson

Neptune may initially seem like an ideal place in which to reside, especially if you're a fading movie star or an unscrupulous real-estate mogul looking for sun, surf, and socialites. Scratch the surface, though, and Neptune begins to look significantly less attractive, even *if* you have the right contacts and a big enough checkbook to get invited to all the best parties. Veronica Mars's hometown harbors a whole range of social ills: petty—and not so petty—crime, racial prejudice, class conflict, political corruption, and Madison Sinclair. Neptune is hardly the ocean paradise it may initially appear to be. Among other things, it provides a very poor environment for nurturing trusting relationships. A typical resident of Neptune may quite reasonably be reluctant ever to trust fully his or her neighbors, co-workers, and even closest friends. Thank goodness for reliable security systems and topnotch private investigators!

Of course, Veronica Mars is a far from being a typical resident of Neptune. Despite her protestations, "normal" has never been her watchword. But Veronica is atypical in ways that should make her even *less* trusting than others in Neptune. Her formative years were, in her own words, spent "watching people while they lied to, cheated on, and betrayed each other" ("Witchita

Veronica Mars and Philosophy: Investigating the Mysteries of Life (Which is a Bitch Until You Die), First Edition. Edited by George A. Dunn.
© 2014 John Wiley & Sons, Inc. Published 2014 by Wiley Blackwell.

Linebacker")—and her experience of lying, cheating, and betrayal is hardly limited to the professional sphere. From being abandoned by her mother to being secretly taped "Adam and Eve style, getting familiar" with her boyfriend Stosh "Piz" Piznarski ("The Bitch Is Back"), Veronica has experienced more than her share of deceptions and betrayals. She could easily be forgiven for adopting an attitude of universal mistrust.

Of course, it *seems* that there are some people whom Veronica genuinely trusts—at least some of the time: her father Keith Mars, Wallace Fennel, Cindy "Mac" Mackenzie, Eli "Weevil" Navarro, and, on a less regular basis, Logan Echolls. But are things really as they seem? Of course not. This is Neptune.

"Trust Me"

Before we can decide whether Veronica genuinely trusts anyone, we need to understand what "trust" really means.[1] Like many questions in philosophy, this one isn't as easy to answer as it may initially seem. Let's start by considering what trust is not. *Trusting* others isn't the same as merely *relying* on them. Veronica regularly relies on Mac's technical expertise with computers, as well as on Weevil's rather more specialized skill set; but full-blown trust is a different matter. We rely on inanimate objects to perform their functions well and to help us in a variety of ways—where would Veronica be without her Taser?—but we don't really trust them in the same sense in which we can be said to trust people.[2] Similarly, we can rely on other people in a wide variety of ways, without ever really trusting them. We can always rely on Richard "Dick" Casablancas, Jr. to be a shallow and sleazy bully; but he's hardly a paradigm of trustworthiness. Nor is relying on someone to act in ways that serve your interests the same as trusting that person. Weevil's information about the fighting Fitzpatrick's narcotics business may ensure that they're "watching his back," but it would take someone much more gullible—and likely soon to be much more dead!—than Weevil ever to *trust* Liam Fitzpatrick ("Nevermind the Buttocks").

Philosophers exploring the nature of trust commonly accept that there's a distinction between trusting and merely relying on others to act in expected ways. It's often observed that we may reasonably feel "let down," even betrayed, when those we trust don't live up to our expectations, but there's no sense of betrayal if we were merely relying on them. According to popular philosophical folklore, the great German philosopher Immanuel Kant (1724–1804) was about as extreme a creature of habit as you'd ever hope to meet, so much so that the other inhabitants of Königsberg, his hometown in East Prussia, used to set their watches by his daily walks. On one occasion he failed to keep to his usual routine and many townsfolk feared that he had died![3] Reliant as the townspeople may have been on Kant's prodigious regularity, Annette Baier (1929–2012) points out that there was no relationship of trust between them and the philosopher.

> The trusting can be betrayed, or at least let down, and not just disappointed. Kant's neighbors who counted on his regular habits as a clock for their own less automatically regular ones might be disappointed with him if he slept in one day, but not let down by him, let alone had their trust betrayed.[4]

Similarly, no matter how much Veronica may rely on her Taser, she could never reasonably feel betrayed if it were to suddenly malfunction. Likewise, if Dick were to visit the wizard and receive a real-life human heart to replace the wadded-up *Maxim* magazine that, Veronica speculates, currently occupies his chest cavity ("There's Got to Be a Morning after Pill"), his improved behavior may shock us and defy our expectations, but it would hardly constitute a betrayal. And if Liam were to forget his agreement with Weevil or to let his temper get the better of him—he was never the most level-headed of people—this would likely cause all manner of problems for Weevil, but a sense that Liam had betrayed his trust would not be among those woes.

So what accounts for our hurt feelings when our trust is violated? A promising answer (pardon the pun) is that trust requires something like a promise or a commitment. According to contemporary philosopher Katherine Hawley, to trust someone to perform a particular action is to "believe that she has a commitment to doing it, and to rely upon her to meet that commitment";[5] and to trust someone in a more general sense is to rely on that person to "fulfill whatever commitments she may have."[6] Commitments can, of course, take many forms. Some are explicit, such as the contract between a private investigator and her clients, the wedding vows exchanged by spouses (which can be the prelude to a contract with a private investigator when someone suspects that those vows are being betrayed), and my promise to meet a group of friends to watch a movie (such as the new one about a private investigator, starring Kristen Bell). Other commitments are unspoken, and thus just implied. It's very unlikely that Tad Wilson ever explicitly promised Carmen Ruiz that he wouldn't spike her drink with gamma-hydroxybutyric acid (GHB), record her *in flagrante delicto* with a popsicle, and then use the video to blackmail her ("M.A.D."). It's equally unlikely that Lianne Mars ever entered into a formal agreement not to steal money from her family ("Leave It to Beaver"). Nonetheless, there was an implicit commitment in both cases, which is why the actions of Tad and Lianne constitute betrayals.

"Who's Your Daddy?"

Now that we're a little clearer about what it means to trust someone, let's return to our central question: Does Veronica trust anyone?[7] Wallace may be her "best friend forever" ("Ruskie Business"), and the story of her romance with Logan may be "epic"—at least in Logan's drunken estimation

("Look Who's Stalking")—but we all know who's the most important person in Veronica's life. Keith Mars is her daddy and he has the paternity test to prove it! It would seem that her relationship with Keith would be the best place to look for a genuinely trusting relationship in Veronica's life. What should we make of their relationship?

It is, in many respects, an extraordinarily close one. You don't need to have scored a 97 (or even a still perfectly respectable 95) on your private investigator's test to figure *that* out. When Veronica was forced to choose between her 09-er friends, with all their wealth and social cachet, and her publicly disgraced former sheriff father, her decision was a foregone conclusion. Veronica sided with Keith and never (well, very rarely) looked back. And her devotion is by no means a one-way street. At the close of "The Bitch Is Back," Keith deliberately destroys evidence to protect his daughter, almost certainly depriving himself of the special election and violating his treasured professional ethics.[8] Nor is Keith's dedication to his daughter evident only at dramatic and life-changing moments. Our many glimpses into what goes on in the Mars household open a window on one of the closest father–daughter relationships on television, albeit one that's unconventional in many ways. So why would I want to spoil Keith's precious "daddy–daughter time" ("The Wrath of Con") by raising the possibility that their relationship might not be one of mutual trust?

It's important to remember that trust is not an all or nothing affair. I might trust someone as a doctor but not as a friend, or trust him to keep a date for coffee but not to return a book. Dean Cyrus O'Dell might still trust Hank Landry in his professional capacity as a criminology professor, even after discovering how untrustworthy Professor Landry is when it comes to the marriage bond. I certainly don't mean to suggest that there is *no* trust between Keith and Veronica. It's clear that there is. Veronica trusts Keith to provide for the family, to track down bail-jumpers, not to abandon her as Lianne has, and for much else besides. Keith trusts Veronica to run the office when he's away and to assist him with many investigations, provided that she takes Backup. The trust between them isn't perfect, however. Keith isn't always so trusting of Veronica when it comes to her "gentleman callers"—though his distrust of Veronica pales by comparison to his wariness of the "gentlemen" themselves. For her part, Veronica doesn't trust Keith to behave honorably in his relationship with Harmony Chase. But isn't perfection too high a standard to expect? Nobody is completely trusting in every respect—or completely trustworthy, for that matter. If the distrust in the Mars household were confined to just a few isolated incidents, my suggestion that their relationship isn't in general one of mutual trust would surely be in error. Sadly, the distrust between father and daughter goes much deeper than that. But don't take my word for it. Let's hear what Veronica has to say on the subject.

"Our Own Game of Spy vs. Spy"

In "Return of the Kane," Veronica wearily describes the dynamic of her current relationship with her father as being "like our own game of Spy vs. Spy." She knows that her father is still investigating Lilly Kane's murder, and he knows that Veronica is doing the same; but, instead of discussing the case and pooling their resources, they spend their time tracking each other's movements, playing games with safe combinations, and spinning cover stories that neither of them believes (doesn't Neptune high school assign the strangest projects?). Their relationship at this point is based less on trust and more on mutual surveillance.[9] To her credit, Veronica recognizes what a sad state of affairs this is. "I don't want things to be like this between us anymore," she confesses to Keith. But, although she clearly wants to end the game, the Spy vs. Spy dynamic persists throughout their relationship. Consider again Keith's behavior in "The Bitch Is Back."[10]

Covering up Veronica's crimes is a remarkable act of love, but not one of trust. Veronica is determined to hide from her father her investigation of the secret organization called The Castle (albeit without much success), while Keith is just as determined to prevent her from discovering what he knows about her activities and the lengths to which he's gone to keep her illegal shenanigans secret.

Veronica may trust Keith (and certain others) in many ways, but her dueling detectives games with her father illustrate two crucial respects in which she is unable to trust anyone. By nature (or, more precisely, by second nature[11]) and by vocation she's unable to rely completely on someone's word, nor will she allow even her most intimate confidants the luxury of having secrets. Of course, Keith can't really complain about Veronica's distrustful nature, since in this (as in so many other respects) she's her father's daughter. After all, tracking your daughter's phone is *not* a sign of trust. But some of the other men in Veronica's life are better placed to take issue with her lack of trust. And, boy, do they!

Veronica's inability to accept other people's word or permit them their secrets is on prominent display when Logan begs her to trust him and not to press for details about his alibi for Mercer Hayes. "I'm not built that way," she explains ("Of Vice and Men"). Of course, Logan is well aware that merely taking him at his word is not something that Veronica is equipped to do. "When have you ever not wanted to know something?" he asks in his inimically brooding fashion ("Of Vice and Men"). Of course, in many ways Veronica is a true blue partner to Logan. She goes above and beyond what can be expected, all to help him clear Mercer's name (at least until she uncovers conclusive evidence of his guilt), and even to protect the duo's secrets. But there's a catch. She'll get Mercer out of jail, she'll keep the police and other interested parties from learning of his and Logan's Mexican misadventures, and she'll even forgive Logan's past transgressions; but all of this has to happen on her terms.

"No one has to know where you were that night," she says, "no one except me" ("Of Vice and Men").

And what if Veronica doesn't trust anyone entirely? What would she gain from having genuinely trusting relationships, anyway? We might doubt that trust is necessarily a good thing. Veronica's world, like our own, often seems to reward suspicion and to punish those who are too trusting. Consider Mac's betrayal by Cassidy "Beaver" Casablancas, or Kendall Casablancas's ill-fated reunion with Cormac Fitzpatrick: both are the consequence of misplaced trust. And Veronica's mistrust is frequently vindicated, as illustrated by the later revelations about Mercer—not to mention what she learns about the actions of those she previously regarded as friends on the fateful night of Shelley Pomeroy's party.[12] If she simply accepted what she was told and resisted the urge to dig around in the dark corners of people's lives, countless crimes in Neptune would have gone unsolved—and most of the show's storylines would have been considerably less interesting. On a professional level, a private investigator who placed a premium on people's privacy and took at face value a suspect's assurances that he wasn't cheating on his spouse or embezzling money from his boss would soon be looking for a new line of work. So, given the obvious risks involved in trusting someone completely, what can be said in its favor?

"I Never Would Have Believed It Either"

To see how Veronica is harmed by her lack of trust, consider a character who is in some respects the anti-Veronica: Meryl, the long-distance girlfriend of Billy "Sully" Sullivan ("On Vice and Men"). Meryl's defining feature is her unshakable confidence in Sully's honesty, fidelity, circle-drawing ability, and all-around wonderfulness. Unfortunately for Meryl, her knight in shining armor has disappeared and is nowhere to be found. Fret not, though, because Veronica Mars is on the case.

As Meryl and Veronica uncover information concerning Sully's disappearance, they're both quick to assume the worst, though in very different ways. Sully has failed to live up to several important (explicit and implicit) commitments: he failed to meet Meryl as agreed, left her no indication of his whereabouts, and isn't responding to her many calls and messages. To Veronica, this is a clear demonstration that Sully is unworthy of the trust that Meryl has placed in him. He's "just another on the list of men who disappoint."[13] Meryl sees it differently, though. Utterly convinced of Sully's trustworthiness, she reckons that the only reason why he wouldn't live up to his commitments must be that he has been rendered unable to undertake them, most likely as a result of some terrible calamity. As the evidence mounts—the revelation of his recent fight with Meryl, his appointment with a suspiciously attractive and well-dressed "study buddy," and the incriminating charges on his credit card—the difference between the beliefs of the two women regarding him becomes even more stark. It is easy to think, along with Veronica, that "you can choose to be a patsy or you can choose not to be," that Meryl is naïve, and that her apparently unrequited devotion to Sully is blinding her to the evidence of his infidelity. However, Meryl sees every bit of evidence that Veronica does. She even acknowledges that, under ordinary circumstances, these facts would be almost infallible signs of an unfaithful jerk, too cowardly to confront his spurned lover. And, when Sully is at last completely exonerated, she displays no bitterness toward Veronica's suspicions, assuring her—with the cutting sincerity available only to the genuinely well-meaning— that "if I hadn't been in love before, I never would have believed it either."[14]

Of course, Veronica's and Meryl's relationship histories are at extreme and opposite ends of the spectrum. Few people have Meryl's good luck to date someone as unassailably trustworthy as Sully. On the other side of the equation, most of us will probably never date someone who had previously organized "bum fights," someone who would later take out a hit on another person, or someone who would later auction stolen sex tapes. (The less said about two-timing drug dealer Troy Vandegraff the better—duplicitous, evil water under the bridge).[15] It's hardly fair, then, for Logan to blame Veronica's inability to trust him entirely on her own suspicious nature. Those who want to be the recipients of unwavering trust should try to be significantly more trustworthy than Logan has shown himself to be. So let's look at someone with a better, albeit briefer, track record: Piz.

As far as Veronica can tell by the end of the show's run, Piz is a real "salt of the earth" kind of a guy.[16] And we've been given no reason so far—aside from a leaked sex tape that he's ultimately shown to have nothing to do with—to doubt that Piz is the standup guy he appears to be. But it's this "so far" that's the problem. To the Meryls of this world, Piz's white hat-wearing credentials would have been firmly established; but to Veronica the nature of Piz's character still remains an open question. When the tape of their amorous activities turns up online, she may not jump to the same conclusion that Logan rather violently does, but she still feels compelled to ask Piz if it's his doing ("Weevils Wobble but They Don't Go Down"). No matter how close her relationships may be, Veronica will always have one eye open, looking for that telltale clue or missing puzzle piece that will reveal that her partner, parent, or friend isn't what he or she seems to be. And it's here that the true cost of her lack of trust lies.[17]

Much of what we value in relationships with those we hold dear has to do with being able to let our guard down around them, in order to establish what contemporary philosopher Laurence Thomas calls bonds of "revealing trust."[18] We share secrets with them, without anyone having to be bullied or blackmailed. Moreover, we take them at their word when they tell us that something is the case. Undoubtedly there's more to a successful friendship than sharing secrets and believing what we're told—and still more to a successful romantic relationship—but without these basic elements we could never truly relax or "be ourselves" around anyone. Like Veronica, we would always be waiting for the other shoe to drop. Of course, this kind of trust also leaves us open to often incredibly painful forms of betrayal—as the younger, more trusting Veronica discovered through her relationship with her mother. But there's no way to avoid these risks while still reaping the benefits that trust affords. Once you've shelled out five grand to a private investigator for the platinum package, no matter what you find out about your partner, the opportunity to trust him or her will have long since passed ("Green Eyed Monster").

Acknowledgment

Thanks to George Dunn and James South for numerous helpful comments on earlier versions of this chapter.

Notes

1. For an excellent general introduction to issues of trust, see Katherine Hawley, *Trust: A Very Short Introduction* (Oxford: Oxford University Press, 2012).
2. Of course, we sometimes talk as if we trust inanimate objects, but this is just a little harmless anthropomorphism, like when we claim that storm clouds look angry or that our computers hate us (actually I'm not convinced that the last one isn't literally true…).
3. He was indeed alive, just inordinately engrossed in Jean-Jacques Rousseau's (1712–1778) philosophical novel *Émile*.
4. Annette Baier, "Trust and Antitrust," *Ethics*, 96.2 (1986): 231–260, at 235.
5. Katherine Hawley, "Trust, Distrust and Commitment," *Nous*, 48.1 (2014): 1–20, at 10.

6. Ibid., 16.
7. I say "a little clearer" because I do not mean to suggest that Hawley's account identifies all the necessary features of trusting someone. In particular, as George Dunn has suggested to me, many believe that what motivates someone to fulfil his or her commitments does matter. Veronica's "go to idea" of blackmailing people ("Poughkeepsie, Tramps and Thieves") may be, among other things, an excellent method for ensuring that these people meet their commitments; but it isn't a method for making them trustworthy.
8. Keith has occasionally broken (or at least bent) his professional code of ethics in other circumstances, his failure to blow the whistle on Deputy Leo D'Amato in "One Angry Veronica" being one such instance. Yet the most severe violations, such as threatening Aaron Echolls in "Rat Saw God" and impeding an FBI manhunt in "Donut Run," are almost invariably motivated by a desire to protect his daughter.
9. As we will see later, close and trusting relationships typically carry with them an implicit commitment to honesty and openness.
10. Examples of similar behavior can be found in "Ruskie Business" and "Donut Run" (among many other episodes).
11. Those influenced by Aristotle (384–322 BCE) use the phrase "second nature" to refer to certain deeply ingrained habits, such as Veronica's habit of digging into the secrets of those around her, or Jackie Cook's habit of spinning elaborate lies concerning her supposedly glamorous New York background.
12. It is worth noting that one of the very few things that can be said in defence of Madison Sinclair's behavior toward Veronica at the party (and in general) is that it does not constitute a betrayal of trust. Madison's "friendly" sartorial advice in "Poughkeepsie, Tramps and Thieves" notwithstanding, it's quite clear that, no matter how long ago we look, the two of them never used to be friends.
13. Veronica actually uses this phrase with reference to Professor Landry; but it is pretty clear that she would consider it an apt description of Sully as well.

14. This is not to deny that there are some severe flaws in Meryl's reasoning: her willingness to jump to conclusions concerning space lasers and sinister forces is more than a little unsettling. For more on Meryl's flawed reasoning, see Chapter 14, by Daniel A. Wilkenfeld, and Chapter 15, by Andrew Zimmerman Jones, in this volume.

15. The actions of Logan Echolls in "Return of the Kane," Duncan Kane in "Not Pictured," and Leo D'Amato in "One Angry Veronica," respectively. Troy's misdeeds are revealed in "You Think You Know Somebody."

16. Piz describes the people of his hometown this way in "Welcome Wagon," and Logan uses the expression, though somewhat insincerely, to describe Piz in "Weevils Wobble but They Don't Go Down."

17. I do not mean to suggest that it is the only cost. Without doubt, there will be others, as recent work on the nature of testimony, for example, has amply illustrated; see Paul L. Harris, "Checking Our Sources: The Origins of Trust in Testimony," *Studies in History and Philosophy of Science* 33.2 (2002), 315–333.

18. Laurence Thomas, "The Character of Friendship," in Damian Caluori, ed., *Thinking about Friendship: Historical and Contemporary Philosophical Perspectives* (New York: Palgrave MacMillan, 2013), 30–46.

Part IV
VERONICA MARS IS NO LONGER THAT GIRL

INVESTIGATING WOMEN IN SOCIETY

Veronica's Trip to the Dentist
Don't Blame the Victim

James Rocha and Mona Rocha

When Veronica Mars asks Madison Sinclair why she wrote "slut" on Veronica's car at Shelly Pomeroy's party, Madison replies: "Because 'whore' had too many letters" ("A Trip to the Dentist"). Madison's words are even crueler than she realizes, since Veronica was raped at that party—not that Madison would ever believe that Veronica was drugged and taken advantage of. Dick Casablancas, who made out with Veronica at that party, doesn't believe her either. When Veronica confronts him about the possibility that he drugged her, he responds: "Don't go blaming me because you got all wasted and slutty" ("A Trip to the Dentist"). Dick's suggestion is that Veronica alone is to blame for whatever happened to her that night.

Veronica had crashed Shelly Pomeroy's 09-er party even though she was neither invited nor welcome. Duncan Kane had broken up with her, leaving her without 09-er credentials. But Veronica came anyway, "just to show everyone that their whispers and backstabbing didn't affect me." Later she admitted that that "was a mistake" ("Pilot"). There are differing accounts of what happened that night. Some, like Dick, say she acted pretty slutty. Others, like Casey Grant, report that boys at the party simply took advantage of her extreme inebriation and lack of

Veronica Mars and Philosophy: Investigating the Mysteries of Life (Which is a Bitch Until You Die), First Edition. Edited by George A. Dunn.
© 2014 John Wiley & Sons, Inc. Published 2014 by Wiley Blackwell.

control. It's hard to tell what really happened, since we can only piece the story together from the conflicting memories of mostly unreliable informants.

Any way you slice it, though, the only reason why Veronica was acting so oddly was that she had been drugged. She took a drink, with no idea of what was in it or who gave it to her. Random alcohol was there for the taking and Veronica downed it. As it turns out, the drink came from Madison, who was unaware that her boyfriend, Dick, had drugged it with gamma-hydroxybutyric acid (GHB), hoping the drug would make her more compliant sexually. The GHB, of course, came from Logan Echolls, who had brought it so that he and his friends could "just have some fun" ("A Trip to the Dentist"). While drugged, Veronica had sex for the first time, though it's not until late in the first season that she learns it was with Duncan Kane, whom Logan had secretly drugged with the same GHB. And, as she learns at the conclusion of the second season, later that night Cassidy "Beaver" Casablancas raped her.

Veronica certainly made mistakes that night. She wasn't invited to the party and she knew that she wasn't welcome there. She took a strange drink, not knowing its origin or contents. Does that make Veronica partially responsible for the horrible things done to her that night? Can we blame her, even in part, for what she suffered?

Walking over Veronica's Corpse for Free Gum

Even questioning Veronica's role in these events raises the issue of what's called "victim blaming": the unfair indictment of the victim. The problem with "victim blaming" is that it fails to acknowledge the victimization and shifts the blame away from the perpetrator, implying that the victim in some way deserved what she got or was responsible for making it happen. Victim blaming is obviously a serious matter, so let's take a close look at how responsibility ought to be assigned in a situation like Veronica's.

Before addressing the issue of Veronica's responsibility, though, we need to answer an important objection. Cassidy is the one who actually raped Veronica, so doesn't he deserve 100 percent of the blame? Of course! Cassidy *is* fully to blame. But that doesn't necessarily let everyone else off the hook. Responsibility and blame aren't zero-sum reckonings, such that adding to one person's blame automatically subtracts it from someone else's. Cassidy remains fully to blame for what he did, but others who contributed to the rape may deserve blame as well.

One key factor in analyzing moral responsibility is determining the causal relationship between acts and outcomes. For someone to be responsible for a bad outcome, he or she must have done something that contributed causally to that outcome in some way. For example, it doesn't make sense to assign any responsibility for Lynn Echolls's suicide to her son Logan, since none of his actions appears to have any direct causal connection to her suicide. It makes more sense to blame Aaron Echolls, since his adultery appears to have contributed directly to his wife's suicide. But, while some causal link is usually necessary before we can hold someone morally responsible for something, a causal connection alone isn't enough.

Consider Parker Lee's rape at Hearst College. After the rape, Parker's mother responds to her daughter's indecision about which wig to wear by admonishing: "You can't make a decision for yourself. This is why you never should have gone away to college: you're too immature" ("My Big Fat Greek Rush Week"). Parker's mom seems to be talking only about wigs, but her words may imply something more, namely that, if immature Parker hadn't chosen to go away to college, she would never have been raped. Of course, it's true that she couldn't be raped at Hearst if she didn't go to Hearst. Her choice to go to Hearst *was* causally connected to her rape, but it doesn't make any sense to hold her responsible for being victimized, since she had no way of knowing that her choice would lead to that outcome.

This brings us to a second condition that must be met before we can assign moral responsibility: the person must have known—or at least *should* have known—that her actions were likely to have the negative outcome they had.

Things don't look good for Veronica when we bring this second condition to bear on her choices. After all, she was drinking an unknown substance at a party where she had known enemies. "There were about a hundred people at Shelly's party," she notes. "Ninety-eight of them would walk over my corpse for free gum" ("A Trip to the Dentist"). Shouldn't she have been more cautious? And, if she acted recklessly, shouldn't she take responsibility for what happened?

"Your Basic Rum, Coke, and Roofie"

But there's another factor to take into account, one that comes to light when we consider the culpability of some of the other partygoers whose actions put Veronica in a position to be raped. She wouldn't have been raped, if not for Logan's buying the GHB. Moreover, she wouldn't have been raped if Dick hadn't drugged Madison's drink, or if Madison hadn't handed her spit-spiked drink to Veronica and given her a "trip to the dentist." And let's not forget how Dick and Sean Friedrich placed a nearly unconscious Veronica on a bed and then goaded Cassidy to rape her. All of these people contributed to Veronica's rape. Before we assess Veronica's responsibility, let's consider to what extent we should blame these other partygoers who in one way or another abetted the rape.

The causal connection is clear, but could any of these characters have reasonably foreseen the harm to which their actions contributed? Consider slipping someone GHB—or any other drug—without telling her about it. Someone who drugs another person certainly bears a great deal of responsibility for the eminently foreseeable bad outcome. Suppose Dick's plan worked as intended: after he slipped GHB to Madison, she would have slept with him. There's a good chance that Madison wouldn't have been interested in having sex with Dick otherwise. After all, when his friend Luke remarks on how hot Madison is, Dick observes that girlfriends are "much like fake boobs, you know. Great to look at, but they don't do as much as you'd like them to" ("A Trip to the Dentist").

In most jurisdictions in the United States, Dick's action—using deception to get Madison to ingest a drug, so that he could have sex with her—would count as rape under the law, even if he used no further deception to obtain sex.[1] The law thus captures something morally intuitive: someone who's being deceived or whose judgment is impaired due to alcohol or drugs isn't genuinely able to consent to sex, since consent implies a clearheaded understanding of the situation and the capacity to decline if one so chooses. Madison can't consent to sex when she's tricked into taking a drug that makes her more willing to engage in sexual activity than she would otherwise be. So, if she had sex with Dick after he drugged her, he would be guilty of raping her—he would have been morally blameworthy and legally culpable.

It's not clear why our assessment of Dick should change just because the person raped is Veronica instead of Madison. Of course, Dick didn't intend to drug Veronica, but he did intend to drug *someone*. He also didn't set out to have sex with Veronica (though, on most accounts of the evening, he did actively flirt with her). Still, he did intend to have sex with a drugged woman. It just so happens that Dick's action results in *another* man's having sex with *another* drugged woman. His intentions are realized in almost every detail—except for the people involved! Dick's actions and their terrible consequences stem from his bad intentions. Dick may not be the one who ultimately raped Veronica, but he intentionally created a situation where a woman would be taken advantage of in a drunken state. So he deserves a lot of blame.

We can now identify three factors in determining someone's responsibility: a causal connection between some action and some outcome; the agent's knowledge of the causal connection; and that same agent's intentions. Let's see how the other party-goers involved measure up by these criteria.

The Road to Hell is Paved with GHB

In Logan's case, intention is more difficult to pin down. He was the one who obtained the GHB. He should have known—and most likely did know—that it could and possibly would be used by his friends to induce others into non-consensual sex. Of course, there's an outside chance that he didn't realize how immoral this action was, but at his age he's responsible for knowing that. He can't escape responsibility by claiming ignorance.

Still, there's an important difference between Dick and Logan's intentions. Logan's stated intention in procuring the GHB was just to have "fun," not "sex with unconscious people fun," as Veronica puts it, but more "like go to a rave fun" ("A Trip to the Dentist"). Assuming that he intended for his friends to use the GHB only on consenting persons, perhaps his purpose in buying and distributing the drug was morally permissible. The terrible consequences of his action were completely contrary to his intentions: he intended something permissible, but something horrible resulted instead. Dick, on the other hand, intended something morally bad, which he achieved, albeit in a different way from the one he had in mind. We are right to assign more blame to Dick.

But Logan's not entirely off the hook. The rape would not have occurred if he hadn't supplied the drugs, and he should have known that something like this could have happened. Good intentions can lead to bad consequences and, if those con-sequences are foreseeable, we're still responsible for them. Logan is negligent in that he fails to see where his intentions could lead. Indeed he bears some of the blame for Veronica's rape, since he's the one who bought and handed out the drugs.

Let's now consider Madison. When she gave Veronica a "trip to the dentist," her intentions were definitely bad, but she had no *knowledge* that she was handing Veronica a drug-laced drink. She only intended to trick Veronica into drinking spit, which is disgusting, but not something that usually causes serious harm. What happened to Veronica shouldn't be blamed on Madison, since she had no way of knowing. Contrary to Veronica's own assessment, Logan is actually more blameworthy than Madison. Even though his intentions may not be not as bad, Logan could have foreseen how a rape may result from supplying his friends with the "rape drug," as GHB is known. Madison, on the other hand, is guilty of only a minor wrong with unforeseeable consequences. If we assign Madison any responsibility (for the rape, that is—she gets full responsibility for the spit), it would have to be very little.

At this point, Dick makes a repeat visit to our rogues' gallery, now in the company of his accomplice Sean. According to Casey's account, Sean and Dick fed a drugged Veronica shots (though Sean insists it was only Dick who did that). The pair then brought her to a bedroom (though Dick insists they only found her there), where, according to Sean and Cassidy, Dick goaded Cassidy into raping her, describing the unconscious Veronica as "a perfectly cute piece of ass, ready and willing" ("A Trip to the Dentist").

Sean, and especially Dick, put Cassidy in a situation that ultimately led to his raping Veronica. The causal connection is quite clear. Moreover, if Sean and Dick claim that they didn't realize the probable consequences of goading a young boy into raping a girl, then their ignorance is clearly blameworthy. The only remaining question concerns their intentions. Were they only joking around? It doesn't appear so in any of the flashbacks. Though we don't have a fully reliable version of what happened, it appears that they really did intend to goad Cassidy into raping

Veronica. It doesn't matter if they claim to have not known that sex with an unconscious woman is rape, since that's something they surely *should* have known at their age.[2] Consequently, Sean and Dick deserve a great deal of blame.

"It Was a Mistake"

Now that we understand what sort of conditions must be met in order properly to hold someone responsible for the consequences of her actions, let's return to Veronica. She did two things that are causally related to her rape: she crashed the party and she took the unknown drink. Clearly, she should have known that those actions could have gotten her into trouble, given how many people at the party didn't like her. Any reasonable person could have seen that these actions were unwise, unsafe, and could lead to disaster. Veronica was intentionally crashing a party where she was not only uninvited, but also unwelcome. But her intentions—to show everyone that their "backstabbing" didn't affect her—were not in themselves morally objectionable, at least not in any big way. And, on a scale of wrongness, crashing a party ranks somewhere below spitting into someone's drink. Since that spit doesn't cast a lot of responsibility on Madison, the same would apply to Veronica's crashing the party.

But, even if Veronica's intentions weren't all that bad, their causal connection to the rape and her knowledge that she was courting trouble seem to be sufficient to assign her some high degree of responsibility. Usually, if someone acts in a way that she knows—or reasonably *should* know—could lead to a disaster, we hold her to some extent responsible for that outcome. Her knowledge, after all, should have deterred her from taking that dangerous action.

Things aren't so simple, though, when it comes to victims. We want to avoid the sort of "victim blaming" that we described earlier, in which the perpetrator is let off the hook. On the other hand, we can't say that victims should never be blamed for their actions, since sometimes their actions are blameworthy. Imagine what might have happened if Veronica had taken that drink and drove home immediately instead of remaining at the party. She could have crashed her car when the GHB kicked in. In that case, she would have been a victim, since she was given the drug without her knowledge; but she would still be largely responsible for the accident, since she should have known better than to take that drink. In addition, if she hurt others due to her thoughtless choice, she would be responsible for the harm done to them too.

What makes Veronica's actual case different is that she doesn't hurt others. She made some stupid choices that were causally linked to a serious harm to herself; but, unlike in our hypothetical scenario, she put only herself in harm's way. Her choices were bad, but only in a *prudential* fashion, meaning that she wasn't thinking enough about her own welfare and the harms to which she was exposing herself. But a prudential mistake that harms only oneself isn't the same thing as a moral lapse that harms others. As bad as her choices were, she didn't violate any of her moral duties to others. We can't assign moral blame for prudential mistakes.

However, matters are complicated if we accept the moral philosophy of the great German thinker Immanuel Kant (1724–1804), who insisted that we have moral duties not only to others, but also to ourselves. In particular, Kant believed that each person has a moral duty to pursue her own moral perfection. Since being an effective moral agent requires using reason, the duty to pursue moral perfection means that Veronica should never do anything that could diminish her ability to act rationally.[3] Excessive drinking, drug use, and even overeating violate a person's duty to oneself, according to Kant, because these actions could cause one to lose control of oneself, diminish one's rational powers, and even lead to addictions that could impair one's ability to make rational choices over the long term.[4] Bear in mind, however, that we have these duties to ourselves *not* because loss of rational control undermines our ability to procure or promote our own happiness.[5] Drunkenness may cause us to make bad prudential choices that impact our happiness, but we don't have a duty to be happy. Rather, we have a duty to safeguard our capacity to make rational choices because we're obligated to respect ourselves as creatures with a rational will.

Admittedly, Veronica took only one drink, but she didn't know what was in it and therefore couldn't know how it would affect her. So perhaps she violated her duty to herself by endangering her ability to exercise self-control and make rational choices. But, even if she's morally blameworthy for taking that drink, that doesn't mean she can be blamed (morally) for her rape. It's true that taking that drink is causally linked to her rape, but the causal connection isn't relevant to whether she violated her duty to herself. If taking the drink was morally wrong, it's wrong regardless of what might happen later.

In short, it doesn't make sense to assign moral blame to a victim for harms that result from prudential mistakes. If someone like Veronica makes a bad prudential choice that causes her harm, then maybe she should blame herself, but we can't blame her for any moral wrong done to her as a result. As a victim, Veronica deserves our sympathy, not our blame. She may have acted foolishly, but that was within her rights. The other partygoers we've considered, however—Madison, Dick, Sean, Logan, and especially Cassidy—are guilty of moral wrongs that caused harm to others.

So, Dick, your protests aside, we will indeed "go blaming" *you* for your bad behavior and its consequences, instead of blaming Veronica, your victim.

Notes

1. Joshua Dressler, *Understanding Criminal Law* (Lexis/Nexis-Matthew Benders Publishers, 2006), 398–404.
2. However, in one study, 88% of males who acted in ways that legally merited rape charges did not consider themselves to have committed rape. See Robert Jensen, *Getting Off: Pornography and the End of Masculinity* (Cambridge: South End Press, 2007), 48–49.
3. Immanuel Kant, *Metaphysics of Morals*, in the *Practical Philosophy* volume of the Cambridge Edition of Immanuel Kant's Works, ed. and trans. Mary J. Gregor (Cambridge: Cambridge University Press, 1996), 516–519.
4. Ibid., 550–552.
5. Ibid., 519–520.

"Grow a Sense of Humor, You Crazy Bitch"
Veronica Mars as a Feminist Icon

Kasey Butcher and Megan M. Peters

In "One Angry Veronica," Veronica Mars is called for jury duty in a case involving two 09-er boys accused of beating a young Latina. Thanks to the recommendation of the "captain of industry," who thinks this will provide Veronica with a good "lesson in civic responsibility," she's elected as jury foreman. Veronica initially believes it's an "open-and-shut" case, the evidence supporting acquittal. But the arguments of the "knitting grandmother," a Latina juror, prompt her to reconsider the evidence and the interpretation of the facts initially accepted by other jurors. The more outspoken Veronica becomes, however, the more resistance she encounters from the "captain of industry." He had initially believed her to be a pliable young woman ripe for a civics lesson. But when she refuses to bow to majority opinion and requests "a logical response to the points I've raised," he loses his cool. "Look, Barbie," he snaps, "I've had a belly full of your snide little digs." His choice of "Barbie" as a nickname, along with his condescending tone, reveals that he has grossly underestimated Veronica, solely on the basis of her age and looks. His opposition to Veronica is a direct result of her refusal to play the role he has assigned her.

Veronica Mars and Philosophy: Investigating the Mysteries of Life (Which is a Bitch Until You Die), First Edition. Edited by George A. Dunn.
© 2014 John Wiley & Sons, Inc. Published 2014 by Wiley Blackwell.

Aggressive opposition to outspoken women is all too familiar, in both popular culture and real life. As educators teaching literature and women's studies, we're often faced with female students hesitant to speak their minds because they're afraid of being perceived as snippy, man-hating, and unfeminine shrews, in short, as "feminist killjoys." Veronica's antagonists frequently imply the same thing about her. Of course, the episode title "One Angry Veronica" alludes to the classic movie *Twelve Angry Men*, but it also calls attention to how often Veronica's anger becomes a source of conflict, as well as a force in the service of justice. Veronica may be a feminist killjoy, but she's also the heroine of the series, constantly fighting on behalf of victims of injustice regardless of their gender, class, or race. As shown in her combative exchange with the "captain of industry," she also understands that being feminine doesn't mean being weak. All along the way, she provides us with a wonderful resource for thinking critically about feminist issues in contemporary society.

Coconuts, the Pirate Ship, and PCH-ers

More than most other characters on the show, Veronica is attuned to how issues of gender, class, and race intersect within the corrupt world of Neptune. Take for example her attempt to help Carmen Ruiz, a self-described "coconut"—which, she explains, is "what you get called in Neptune when you're Latino and date white people or join Honor Society" ("Versatile Toppings"). Carmen's an easy target for bullying, since she doesn't fit neatly into either the 09-er community or the Latino community of Neptune. Carmen's relationship with Tad Wilson, a white 09-er on his way to the Naval Academy, prompts Eli "Weevil" Navarro to remark: "Now that's a shame. Neighborhood girl like that, wasting her assets on a white boy" ("M.A.D."). But, despite her perceived disloyalty to the "neighborhood," Carmen doesn't entirely fit in with the 09-ers either, because of her lower socioeconomic status. Recalling Veronica's relationship with Duncan Kane, Carmen's only entrée into 09-er society is through the upper-class boy she dates. Her precarious and ambiguous status at Neptune High results from a complicated intersection of race, class, and gender.[1]

Tad, on the other hand, benefits from his status as a wealthy white heterosexual male. He attempts to blackmail Carmen when she tries to break up with him, threatening to post a video of her miming oral sex with a popsicle. Sympathetic to the nuances of Carmen's predicament, Veronica proposes a plan to blackmail Tad in return, hitting him where it hurts. With the help of Cindy "Mac" Mackenzie, Veronica creates a website to (falsely) expose Tad's having an affair with Seth Rafter, a gay teen he bullied. This would threaten Tad's position at the Naval Academy as well as his status as a heterosexual male in a homophobic high school. Though in this case Veronica weaponizes homophobia, it's worth noting that in other episodes she helps reunite a classmate with his estranged father, now a transgender woman ("Meet John Smith"), and saves gay and lesbian peers from being blackmailed out of the closet ("Versatile Toppings").

Feminist legal theorist Kimberlé Crenshaw has used the term "intersectionality" to describe how race, gender, class, and other identities can intersect to create complex experiences of discrimination.[2] Carmen, for example, is vulnerable on multiple levels, because she is young, lower class, Hispanic, and female. Similarly, when Veronica reports her rape to Sheriff Lamb and he contemptuously suggests that she wants him to round up the sons of all the wealthiest men in Neptune, he highlights Veronica's lower-class status, compounding her disempowerment as a teenage girl ("Pilot"). Many contemporary feminists think that attention to intersectionality offers a corrective to the way feminism has privileged the perspectives and needs of white middle-class women in the past.

One of Veronica's strengths is her ability to connect with other girls across class and racial lines. On the surface, Veronica is the perfect white girl—petite, blonde, clever, sporty, and feminine—but she becomes an outsider after her father's recall from office and her falling out with the 09-ers. Consequently, she can leverage her privilege as a pretty white woman, while still using her status as an outsider to assert her independence. Over the course of the first two seasons, her outsider status is frequently compromised through her friendship with Meg Manning, her relationships with Logan Echolls and Duncan, and her complicated friendship with Weevil. Each of these associations brings her closer to the inside of the 09-ers or of the PCH Bike Club. Still, Veronica remains on the fringe: not totally on the outside, yet unwilling to be an insider, able to use her position on the boundaries to gain knowledge and allies, fight for social justice, and benefit those who lack power within the corrupt systems of Neptune.

"No It Was *You! You* Were Too Much Man!"

Veronica's nuanced understanding of how gender roles are performed often aids in her investigations.[3] Many feminists endorse the theory that gender is at bottom a matter of *performance*, meaning that gender roles are not dictated by biology, but rather are a set of learned behaviors that are culturally and socially acquired. Performing the gender roles deemed appropriate by society is a way to blend in; but we also have the option of flouting those conventions, thereby demonstrating that gender is in fact a performance. Veronica's appreciation of the fluidity of gender roles helps her to steer the expectations of those around her to serve her purposes. She's able to read how people will perceive her and to adjust her performances accordingly—and she often plays against expectations as well.

Many people whom Veronica encounters in her investigations view the 5-foot-nothing pretty blonde teenager as incapable of posing a serious threat, while others go out of their way to impress her. By manipulating and exploiting these expectations, Veronica is often able to gather evidence that might not be offered up to the police, or even to her father, Keith Mars. For instance, while looking for clues as to whether the bus crash that begins the second season was a suicide or an accident, she visits the convenience store where bus driver Ed Doyle made his last phone call. To gather information, she flirts with Duane Anders, the store clerk whom she had seen on television the night before giving an interview that belied his interest in milking his 15 minutes for all they're worth. And her flirtation works! He asks if she's one of the "freaky sex and death type kids," noting that she isn't like the other Goths who've been in the store recently to ask questions about the bus crash: "If we've been getting a lot of Munsters in here, I'd say that you're the Marilyn, hon, 'cause you're pretty." In the process, he provides Veronica with a vital clue, which proves that the accident wasn't a suicide ("Driver Ed").

Veronica engages in another performance of excessive femininity to gain access to Patrick Colin Nevin's house, as part of the $3,000 gold package "temptation scenario" requested by his almost fiancée, Julie Bloch. Outfitted in a short skirt and revealing top, Veronica appears at Colin's door, feigning ignorance of how to change a flat tire. She checks out his body a little too obviously, bends over to draw attention to her derriere, and makes a number of suggestive comments, all in an effort to tempt him into making a pass at her ("Green-Eyed Monster"). Colin doesn't fall for the temptation scenario, but he does recognize that Veronica is giving a "performance," which he reads as the flirtatious behavior of a "girl who knows she's gorgeous, but likes to hear it anyway."

These scenes illustrate what film scholar Mary Ann Doane calls "masquerade," an act of *excessive* femininity that draws attention to gender as a performance.[4] This isn't to say that all women who enact their femininity in this way are being inauthentic, or even that they recognize that what they're doing *is* a performance. The point is simply that women are often socially expected to perform in ways that may not be authentic for them. Veronica's very deliberate performances of over-the-top femininity draw attention to the performative nature of gender in general.

While Veronica exploits the expectations of others via masquerade, she also draws attention to the performance of masculinity, specifically by Logan and Duncan. In "Nobody Puts Baby in a Corner" she recites all of the lines from *The Big Lebowski* along with the film, mimicking Jeff Bridges's stoner slang—much to Duncan's consternation. And in "Driver Ed," while snuggling in bed with Duncan, she playfully pretends to "hock a loogie" onto his neck and mimics the kinds of comments she hears from male jocks. As a soccer player, Duncan would be friends with many young men who behave in the way Veronica calls attention to.

Veronica is also keen on exposing Logan's brand of learned hyper-masculinity. (His father, of course, is a famous action movie star!) After the two of them had evidently been indulging the night before in a Clint Eastwood marathon, we see a shot of Logan reclining on a bench on the Hearst Campus, his arms spread across the back and his legs wide apart, in a distinctly masculine posture. The camera pulls back to reveal Veronica mimicking his pose, which prompts Logan to remark: "Now I've ruined you. I didn't think it was possible to make you more butch." When he suggests that she walk him to class and she offers to carry his books, the playful gender reversal shows not only his posturing, but also her ability to recognize it and tease him about it ("Welcome Wagon"). Her playfulness treats gender roles as fluid identities—to be tried on when they serve some useful purpose or, at times, just to draw attention to their own artifice.

"My Boots Aren't Butch"

Watching Veronica put into practice her understanding of intersectionality and gender performance can give viewers an implicit understanding of some of the important themes of contemporary feminism. It isn't until the third season, however, that the show directly addresses the issue of what feminism means in Neptune. Until the first encounter with the women of Lilith House, it would be difficult to know on what terms Veronica might define herself or how she might fit within the history of feminism. Enter Nish Sweeny, Fern Delgado, and friends.

With Lilith House, we're treated to one of the most stereotypical and damaging portraits of feminists in recent years. All of the women are presented as unjustifiably angry, humorless, and militant, and, with the exception of Claire Nordhouse, all are women of color who don't conform to traditional norms of femininity. Perhaps this stereotype-laden presentation could be ignored, as the women are played off the similarly formulaic brothers of the Pi Sigma house. There's an important difference between the two groups, however, and it is crystalized in their very different relationships to the ongoing rape crisis on the Hearst campus.

The women of Lilith House are actively working to dismantle a campus culture that they believe implicitly encourages and condones rape. They picket the sites of rape, protest at sporting events, and go on Stosh "Piz" Piznarski's radio show to debate the *Hearst Lampoon* editors and denounce them for trivializing the campus rapes on their front page ("Wichita Linebacker"). Their activities are met with little more than exasperated sighs from an unhelpful and unsympathetic Dean Cyrus O'Dell, and they're vilified throughout campus for disrupting the party culture. The women of Lilith House are essentially "feminist killjoys." Meanwhile, the Pi Sig brothers are hell-bent on maintaining the status quo, which serves them so well. They're indifferent to the harms caused by, for instance, the "grope room" in their haunted house ("Charlie Don't Surf") and are unwilling to comply with the dean's mandate that they provide drug-detecting coasters at their events ("Spit & Eggs"). Their failure to comply ultimately leads to Veronica's being drugged and attacked by Mercer Hayes ("Spit & Eggs"), but there seem to be no consequences for the Pi Sigs. Their bad behavior continues, as both Chip Diller and Dick Casablancas send out the "sex tape" of Piz and Veronica. Meanwhile, Lilith is never heard from again, since they've been banned from campus, though Nish shows up in a later episode to give Veronica information about The Castle ("The Bitch is Back").

The women of Lilith House bring to mind what is often referred to as second-wave feminism. Historically, feminism has been understood as moving in three major waves. First-wave feminism, emerging at the turn of the twentieth century, focused on gaining for women the right to vote and own property. Second-wave feminism fought for women's access to education, job equality, and reproductive rights, while rebelling against traditional gender norms. Third-wave feminism— what we call contemporary feminism—is a response to the perceived failures of second-wave feminism. Emphasizing intersectionality and gender performativity, it offers a more inclusive and flexible understanding of what it means to be a woman in American society today. The negative portrayal of Lilith House highlights aspects of second-wave feminism that many young women today seem to resist. Still, it's outrageously hyperbolic and does a real disservice to the progress made by second-wave feminists on behalf of women, the fruits of which are enjoyed by most young women in America today, including Veronica.

Veronica can be seen as a representative of a new type of feminism, which remedies the limitations of the earlier waves. She doesn't dismiss femininity, she has a positive attitude toward sex, and she approaches most issues on a personal rather than just on an outwardly political level. That's not to say that she doesn't see a relationship between the personal and the political—that there *is* such a relationship is a basic tenet of feminism throughout all three waves—but she's unwilling to politicize events until she's come to a full understanding of their nature. She embodies what second-wave feminism—and Lilith House—don't offer: a more fluid understanding of gender performativity, a respect for a diversity of voices and views, and a positive engagement with sexuality that encourages agency and play. Veronica provides a model of contemporary feminism that's not only successful and lauded within the world of Neptune, but also resonant with young viewers.

"A Pamphlet's Not Going to Cover It"

"Sex-positivity" refers to an attitude that separates sexuality from any moral judgment, encouraging acceptance of diverse expressions of sexuality, from abstinence to kink, and celebrating the potential of sexuality to forge positive human connections. It rejects the idea that sexuality is necessarily dangerous, harmful, or shameful, and it emphasizes personal choice and consent while deemphasizing other people's judgments of one's conduct. It refuses to make sexual "purity" the measure of one's value. As in so many other ways, Veronica is exemplary in her sex-positive attitude.

Veronica's emotional distress over her rape and her inability to remember what happened to her that night don't cause her to buy into the notion that she's been ruined by her rape. Instead, she reclaims control of her body and her sexual autonomy, waiting until she feels ready for further sexual activity, while coping with malicious rumors about her supposed sexual promiscuity. She demonstrates that, no matter what her reputation or her prior experiences may be, her decisions about sex and relationships remain her own. Indeed Veronica's struggles help her to sympathize and connect with other girls who have suffered violence or abuse. Among other things, she defends a victim of incest ("The Girl Next Door"), helps to bring down a beloved teacher who's guilty of statutory rape ("Mars vs. Mars"), and attempts to save Carmen from being blackmailed by her boyfriend ("M.A.D.").

Veronica encourages other young women to take control of their sex lives and not to shame others for their personal decisions regarding their sexuality. Characters who *do* engage in "slut shaming"—such as Madison Sinclair, Fern Delgado, and Aaron Echoll's attorney Ethan Lavoie—are all recognizably on the wrong side.[5] At Aaron's murder trial, Lavoie tries to discredit Veronica's testimony by asking her about her treatment for chlamydia and by portraying her as an underage temptress who, like her best friend Lilly, attempted to seduce Aaron ("Happy Go Lucky"). The ruse works and Aaron goes free, illustrating how justice can be derailed when a woman's sexuality is used to shame or discredit her. (Of course, "justice" catches up with Aaron that night.)

Perhaps because of the many ways in which her own reputation has been formed by gossip, victim blaming, and slut shaming, Veronica isn't in the habit of using someone's sexual reputation as a way to bring that person down—her weaponization of homophobia to protect Carmen from Tad notwithstanding—and she doesn't mistake someone's score on a "purity test" for a measure of character ("Like a Virgin"). When she's wrong in her assessment of someone, as she was when she called Carrie Bishop "fast," she offers an apology ("Mars vs. Mars"). She helps those like Carmen, who've had their agency taken away from them, and encourages Mac and Parker Lee to reclaim control of their sexuality after being victimized. In these ways and in many others, Veronica presents a sex-positive model that's distinctly feminist.

Like Veronica, feminism itself is imperfect. It's continually evolving to include the diverse experiences of women—and men—from different backgrounds. Even though the portrayal of the Hearst feminists is lacking in some respects and grossly unfair in others, Veronica's engagement with issues that impact young women opens a space for the sort of conversations that third-wave feminism is all about, conversations that include a diversity of voices. Veronica's sleuthing can instruct us in how to lead an engaged and empowered life that isn't bound by conformity. It isn't easy being so hardboiled—or being a feminist—but it's honest.

Notes

1. For more on how race and class shape the lives of the residents of Neptune, see Chapter 3 in this volume, by Regena Saulsberry.
2. Kimberle Crenshaw, "Mapping the Margins: Intersectionality, Identity Politics, and Violence against Women of Color," *Stanford Law Review*, 43.6 (1991): 1241.
3. For a great discussion of the ways in which Veronica uses gender roles in relationship to both feminism and *noir* tropes, see Andrea Braithwaite, "'That Girl of Yours—She's Pretty Hardboiled, Huh?' Detecting Feminism in Veronica Mars," in Sharon Marie Ross and Louisa Ellen Stein, eds., *Teen Television: Essays on Programming and Fandom* (Jefferson, NC: McFarland, 2008).
4. Mary Ann Doane, "Film and the Masquerade: Theorising the Female Spectator," in E. Ann Kaplan, ed., *Feminism and Film* (Oxford: Oxford University Press, 2004). 426.
5. For more on "slut shaming" and why it's wrong, see Chapter 12 in this volume, by by Jordan Pascoe.

12

On Not Being a Slut (Even When Everyone Thinks You Are)

Jordan Pascoe

"I don't see how you do it. … Deal. The way people talk about you. Does it bother you, the things they say?" cheerleader Meg Manning asks Veronica when Meg's reputation is destroyed by a false score on an online "purity test." "No," replies Veronica. "Here's what you do. You get tough, you get even" ("Like a Virgin").

The purity test scandal highlights a pervasive double standard: reputations shape the lives of just about everyone, but to be declared a slut is to be publicly denied the right to even basic kinds of respect. Whether acquired through roofies, pornified popsicle eating, faked purity test results, or actual promiscuity, a reputation as a slut makes one an object of public derision, something to be toyed with and discarded. And this public slut shaming turns out to be bad not only for the girls accused of being sluts, but for the slut sneezers as well.

Purity, Respect, and Personhood

"I'm actually excited about going to school tomorrow," says Veronica, when she learns that you can buy any Neptune High student's purity test results for $10 a pop. Nearly every student

Veronica Mars and Philosophy: Investigating the Mysteries of Life (Which is a Bitch Until You Die), First Edition. Edited by George A. Dunn.
© 2014 John Wiley & Sons, Inc. Published 2014 by Wiley Blackwell.

has taken the test, which consists of 100 questions covering a range of sexual, moral, and narcotic misdeeds—"everything you could possibly do that's dirty or fun or illegal," as Dick Casablancas puts it. Someone who scores a 90 is pretty pure. Someone with a 12 is going to either hell or reform school. Of course, the results don't mean the same thing for everyone. As 09-er Pam points out during a lunchtime discussion of the purity test: "If you get a 60, you're 60 percent pure, 40 percent sack jockey. Anything under 60's really slutty." "Unless you're a guy," chimes Duncan. If "good" girls are supposed to get high scores, *studly* guys are supposed to get low scores. Guys with low purity scores get bragging rights; girls with low purity scores get called sluts.

When Meg gets to school the day the results are released, the number 48 is plastered across her locker, along with the word "slut." The locker next to hers, however, is marked with a 32 and the words "You're the best!" Either this locker belongs to a girl being mocked for her low score or it belongs to a guy being praised. Veronica doesn't take the test, but a fake score is posted for her anyway—a shamefully low 14, which in her assessment means that people must think she's the biggest slut in school. She teases Wallace Fennel for his score of 70, calling him a "30 percent danger-lovin', girl-touchin' rock star," but in fact 70 is too high for a guy to reap much glory.

The purity test reminds us that sluts and studs aren't terribly different. You get called a "stud" or a "slut" on account of a reputation for being sexually promiscuous. The only difference is that studs are applauded for their reputation, while sluts are shamed for theirs. At Neptune High, a girl with a reputation for being a slut quickly loses the right to speak—or, as Meg learns when auditioning for "Cabaret," even to *sing*—unmolested. When Veronica's teacher Mrs. Murphy asks for her "position" on a topic under discussion, Dick blurts out, "All fours!" In short, girls who are called sluts aren't treated as full-fledged persons deserving of respect. Rather they experience *objectification*, the process by which persons are stripped of their dignity and treated as mere things.

But what exactly does it mean to treat a person as a thing, and why is such treatment wrong? Our present-day understanding of personhood draws heavily on the ideas of the German philosopher Immanuel Kant (1724–1804), who insisted on a sharp distinction between persons and things. Persons are rational beings possessing *autonomy*, the ability to make choices for themselves and set their own ends or goals in life. Not only do persons have ends; they are also, on Kant's view, "ends in themselves," which means that the existence of persons with the capacity to make rational choices is an intrinsically good thing and that we should therefore safeguard both our own *autonomy* and that of others. Persons possess an inherent dignity and are entitled to being treated with respect. Things, on the other hand, exist only to be used or enjoyed by us. You can do whatever you want to a thing, since it has, in itself, no value that we need to respect. We *objectify* a person whenever we treat her like a thing, using her as a mere means to our own ends, while disregarding her right to set goals for herself as an autonomous being.

Using deceit or manipulation to get others to do what we want is one of the most common ways of treating another person as a mere means to our ends. Being deceived interferes with our capacity to act autonomously, since we can't make good choices for ourselves on the basis of false information. In order to achieve her own goals, the deceiver is willing to sacrifice the ability of other people to achieve theirs, something she wouldn't do if she truly respected others as rational beings. Kant would probably be scandalized by how regularly Veronica resorts to deceit and manipulation to get her way. For example, when she flirts with Deputy Leo D'Amato in order to break into the evidence room, she achieves her goal of stealing evidence by manipulating Deputy Leo, even as she undermines his goal of performing his job conscientiously. "Girl uses boy," notes

Veronica in a voiceover, indicating that she at least understands the nature of what she's doing ("Silence of the Lamb").

But using others isn't *always* wrong, according to Kant. When Vice-Principal Clemmons wants Veronica's help in retrieving Polly the Parrot, the school mascot, Veronica tells him that she wants, in return, a parking space, a letter of recommendation, and a different locker. She freely consents to help him achieve his end as long as he helps her to achieve hers ("Betty and Veronica"). Such arrangements of mutual or reciprocal assistance are a regular part of our lives. We may be using each other, but it's all good because no one is being coerced or deceived. The key concept here is *consent*. Each party has voluntarily entered into the arrangement with eyes open and his or her autonomy fully intact.

Kant's ideas on personhood and objectification can help us understand what's wrong with the treatment meted out to girls at Neptune High who get labeled as "sluts." But in order to understand better how Kant's ideas apply, let's first look at another victim of the sexual double standard at Neptune High: Carmen Ruiz.

"What Do You Want for Christmas?" … "Love and Respect"

The humiliation that Veronica and Meg suffer in the wake of the purity test is slight compared to what their classmate Carmen faces when her boyfriend Tad Wilson threatens to publicly post a video of her suggestively sucking a popsicle. If the video goes viral, Carmen worries, "I'll become a national joke!" ("M.A.D."). While Veronica's and Meg's false purity test scores haunt them in the hallways of Neptune High, Carmen's video threatens to humiliate her before a national audience. And so Veronica gives Carmen the same advice she gives Meg: Get even!

Has Tad failed to respect Carmen as a person? Clearly. When he makes the video and threatens to use it to keep her in a relationship, he treats her as a mere means to his end, rather than respecting her as a person with ends of her own. He doesn't care what Carmen wants; he cares only about what *he* wants. Needless to say, Carmen hasn't consented to being manipulated in this way. But that's not all that's at play here. Tad also gave Carmen a dose of gamma-hydroxybutyric acid (GHB) that night, to lower her inhibitions and to weaken her will. It was only by deliberately impairing her capacity for rational judgment that he was able to get her to do the sexy popsicle dance for him in the first place. This involves more than just treating her as a means to an end, someone to be manipulated into helping him get what he wanted. Tad actually sought to reduce Carmen to a mere object of enjoyment—which is layers worse because it's inherently demeaning, as Kant makes us see.[1]

Kant saw sex as a morally problematic drive because it involves a desire to use another person's body for one's own pleasure. Because sex is a desire directly for a *body*, rather than for the *person*, we tend to regard that person as if she were merely an object designed for our pleasure. Consequently, to the extent that our interest in another person is purely sexual, we're not at all interested in her other qualities—her intelligence, her sense of humor, or her capacity to make choices for herself. Like Logan Echolls when he creates his "lowest common denominator" website devoted to female "asses," we value the other individual merely as a sexual object rather than as a person. As Kant puts it,

> the desire a man has for a woman is not directed towards her because she is a human being, but because she is a woman; that she is a human being is of no concern to the man; only her sex is the object of his desires.[2]

What Tad wants when he induces Carmen to dance and suck a popsicle for him isn't Carmen as a *person*. It's her body. That Tad desires Carmen's body and not her person is especially clear from the fact that he drugs her, crippling her capacity for autonomous choice, even as her body becomes more available and more willing. Once she's drugged, she can't consent. Tad is thus in a position to manipulate her into becoming a body designed purely for his pleasure. But this leaves us with the question of whether it would have been okay if, instead of drugging Carmen, Tad had gotten her to freely consent to performing the popsicle dance for his pleasure. From Kant's point of view, Tad would still be treating her as an object, because sex is *always* about objectification, *always* a matter of reducing an autonomous person deserving of respect to an object of pleasure.

Let's admit that this is a pretty bleak view of sex. Fortunately we don't have to agree with everything Kant says on this topic. There may indeed be many instances of sex where the partners still respect each other as persons, where sex is tied to mutual affection and to a deep concern for the other person's well-being. Hopefully this is the kind of sex that Veronica was having with Duncan (after their inauspicious first time) and with Logan. Presumably it's *not* the kind of sex Logan had with Madison Sinclair, which probably fits the Kantian description pretty well. But Kant's inability to imagine loving, respectful sex doesn't mean that we should dismiss all of his arguments out of hand. His claim that sex is objectifying is especially useful when trying to understand why a reputation as a slut is so damaging.

Slut Sneezing

In Neptune, as Carmen and Meg learn, it's girls in particular who are the victims of sexual objectification, who get reputations as sluts, and who therefore get treated as sexual objects. But why should girls in particular be victimized if, as Kant believes, sex objectifies everyone? Why isn't sex an equal-opportunity objectifier, for guys and girls alike? And why does Meg's 48 make her a slut, if the same score would make Dick a stud?

This simple answer is that sex means different things for women and for men, in Neptune and elsewhere. Feminist scholar Catherine MacKinnon has argued that objectification isn't gender-neutral the way Kant thinks it is. Objectification, she argues, is what happens when we *want* someone to be merely an object, when we have the power to *force* that person to behave as an object, and when we derive some sense of pleasure and empowerment from being able to make the world conform to our desires in this way.[3] MacKinnon believes that, generally speaking, men want a world in which women are objects and that men have the power to bring this world about.[4]

Even if this isn't true of all men, it's clear that Neptune is populated by lots of guys who see nothing wrong with reducing women to the status of sexually available objects, regardless of whether the woman in question is conscious. There's Tad, Dick, and their GHB. There's Sean Friedrich, who helped Dick position an unconscious Veronica to be raped by Cassidy "Beaver" Casablancas. And there's the other 09-er, who did body shots off Veronica's near-unconscious body.

MacKinnon reminds us that objectification is intimately tied to power. Each time that Tad, Dick, or anyone else objectifies someone, part of the pleasure they experience has to do with enjoying the power to treat someone else as an object. When Veronica is laid out for Dick and available for body shots, part of his experience consists in feeling that she exists *for him* or that, more generally, the world is organized so that others exist purely for his pleasure. As an object lying there for his pleasure, Veronica doesn't demand his respect or his concern. She simply reminds him that he's powerful and that others exist to give him what he wants.

MacKinnon thinks that this is a quintessentially male experience. To be a man in our culture is to experience one's own power through the objectification of women. And, equally, being a woman is to experience being objectified. Consequently, we live in a world where all men are potential studs and all women are potential sluts. Objectification isn't something that just happens in bedrooms and parked cars. It's tied to larger social forces.

MacKinnon's argument allows us to understand Kant's claims about sex in a different light. If some sex—the non-loving, non-respectful kind—always involves objectification, that doesn't mean that *all* participants are reduced to the status of objects. Rather, MacKinnon suggests that sex produces an *object* and an *objectifier*. And this helps us to make sense of the difference between sluts and studs at Neptune High. Both are sexually promiscuous, but guys get a positive reputation for being virile and powerful. They're studs. For girls, on the other hand, promiscuity—real or imagined—always means being demeaned and treated more as a thing than as a person.

Getting Tough and Getting Even

Kant would agree with MacKinnon that objectification is a social force. This is an additional reason why treating people as things is so morally dangerous. Tad certainly objectifies Carmen when he makes that popsicle video, but he's not the only person who does so. Once the video of her popsicle-sucking dance goes viral, everyone who views it is in a position to objectify Carmen, too. She's presented to the world as an object and, consequently, the world comes to treat her as such. As Carmen and Veronica walk across campus the morning the video is released, a jerk pulls a popsicle out from behind him and taunts, "I thought you might want to suck on my popsicle" ("M.A.D."). His gibe suggests that, if Carmen is willing to suck her boyfriend's popsicle, she must be willing to suck *anyone*'s popsicle. She is, from his perspective, just a popsicle-sucking object, rather than a person with ends of her own.

This is precisely the danger of objectification. Kant worries that, like the video of Carmen, objectification goes viral, so that, "as soon as a person becomes an object of appetite for another … [that] person becomes a thing and can be treated and used as such by everyone."[5] Once Carmen is reduced to the status of an object of Tad's appetite, she's in danger of being seen as such by others. Once she's been reduced to being a popsicle-sucking thing, she must be available to suck anyone's popsicle—or to suck anyone's *anything*, for that matter. That's why a reputation as a slut is so damaging: it's not just about what you *have* done; it's about people's presumptions about what you *would* do. It's about a collective fantasy that a girl who has been promiscuous would be willing to do anything with anyone.

There's a lot of eighteenth-century sexual conservatism in Kant's views, but the conclusion he comes to is strikingly similar to the politics of slut shaming at Neptune High. The problem with sex isn't just sex. It's the way in which the reputation you get for having sex shapes how others think they can treat you. Once Meg's reputation as a slut is in place, other people will treat her that way. They'll make lascivious noises when she auditions for the school play, they'll call her house to say obscene things, and they'll "slut sneeze" as they pass her in the hallway. In short, they'll treat her as an object and fail to respect her as a person. For Kant, this is precisely why sexuality—and, I would argue, "sluttiness"—is such a morally dangerous terrain: in Kant's view we *can't* think about having sex with someone *without* objectifying that person. And so, when someone has a reputation as a slut, that's exactly what happens.

The reputations of Carmen, Veronica, and Meg as sluts are forged entirely from liquid GHB, manipulation, and false test scores. And those who handed them that liquid GHB or that faked a score on the purity test are surely guilty of objectifying them. But that's not all: the Neptune students who taunt, tease, and slut sneeze them are *also* guilty of treating these women as objects and of the deep moral failure of not respecting a person as an end in herself. In any instance of slut shaming, the so-called "slut" is never in the wrong. Even if Meg really had scored a 48 on the purity test, her classmates still would have no right to treat her as a thing—to deride her publicly, call her home mockingly, or cat-call her as she walks down the hall. The problem isn't Meg—it's everyone else.

Disrespect and objectification don't happen in a vacuum. There are bigger social forces at work that make promiscuous guys studs and promiscuous girls sluts. To return to Veronica's advice to Meg—"You get tough, you get even"—it's clear that the culture of objectification at Neptune High is so pervasive that just "get-ting tough" is almost never enough. You have to fight back. As Veronica tells Mandy—a victim of bullying, who had hired Veronica to find her stolen dog: "You want people to treat you with respect? You have to *demand* it" ("Hot Dogs").[6] The default for girls at Neptune High is lack of respect, *not* being treated as someone smart, interesting, and worthwhile. If you want to be treated that way, Veronica is right: you have to demand it.

Notes

1. For more on the immorality of using GHB to lower a prospective sexual partners inhibitions, see Chapter 10 in this volume, by James Rocha and Mona Rocha.
2. Immanuel Kant, *Lectures on Ethics* (Indianapolis, IN: Hackett, 1969), 164.
3. Catherine MacKinnon, *Toward a Feminist Theory of the State* (Cambridge, MA: Harvard University Press, 1989), 122, 137–138. See also Sally Haslanger, "On Being Objective and Being Objectified," in Louise M. Antony and Charlotte E. Witt, eds., *A Mind of One's Own* (Boulder, CO: Westview Press, 2002), 237.
4. Catherine MacKinnon, *Feminism Unmodified* (Cambridge, MA: Harvard University Press, 1987), 50.
5. Immanuel Kant, *The Lectures on Ethics* (Indianapolis, IN: Hackett, 1969), 163.
6. For more on "getting even," see Chapter 7 in this volume, by George A. Dunn.

Part V
VERONICA MARS IS SMARTER THAN ME

INVESTIGATING HOW AND WHY WE INVESTIGATE

"I Used to Think that Solving the Case Was the Key to Our Happiness"
The Value of Truth in *Veronica Mars*

Dereck Coatney

Throughout much of the series, Veronica Mars works for her father Keith Mars's private investigation firm. She uses the investigative know-how she's learned from her "job" to solve various problems she faces, in addition to problems of her friends, and sometimes even of people who are simply willing to pay. And she's really, really good at it too. Most often, Veronica's skillful exercise of her investigative prowess is in the service of discovering and exposing the truth about the situations that she and others are faced with. What else should we expect from a sleuth? We are led to admire the strength and persistence with which she strives to learn the truth behind the frequently miscreant dealings concealed beneath Neptune's glamorous façade.

But is Veronica's uncovering of the truth always something good? Granted, through her pursuit of the truth, she's often able to save her friends from injustices and false accusations. But is the truth always worthy of our praise? Like the truth about so many other things in Neptune, the truth about the truth is hardly that simple.

Veronica Mars and Philosophy: Investigating the Mysteries of Life (Which is a Bitch Until You Die), First Edition. Edited by George A. Dunn.
© 2014 John Wiley & Sons, Inc. Published 2014 by Wiley Blackwell.

"I've Got a Secret … A Good One!"

The value of the truth is one of the most prominent questions considered by the German philosopher Friedrich Nietzsche (1844–1900). Indeed, he begins his well-known book *Beyond Good and Evil* with just this very question. After opening the first chapter with the claim that the "will to truth"—or the desire for truthfulness—is something about which "all philosophers so far have spoken with respect," he suggests that the will to truth has now evolved to the point where it can begin to interrogate the truth about itself. This process begins with an attempt to discover the motivation behind this will, but it also ultimately leads to a "still more basic question. We asked about the *value* of this will. Suppose we want truth: why not rather untruth? and uncertainty? even ignorance?"[1] Nietzsche notes that people regularly insist that they want the truth. But aren't there often good reasons for wanting its opposite, or at least uncertainty or ignorance?

Nietzsche observes that one reason why people believe so much in the value of truth is that they imagine, perhaps mistakenly, that knowing the truth is *useful*. Certainly, most of the clients who walk through the doors of Mars Investigations hope that they can parlay the truths that they pay top dollar to uncover into some kind of advantage for themselves (such as a bigger divorce payout), or that they can at least use those truths to avoid some kind of harm. Harmony Chase wants to know if her husband is cheating on her, so that she'll have a reason to divorce him ("Charlie Don't Surf"). Julie Bloch wants to know whether her boyfriend and potential fiancé Collin Nevin is the gold-digging philanderer she fears he might be, so that she can avoid the mistake of marrying him ("Green-Eyed Monster").

Nietzsche discusses this particular motive for wanting to know the truth—faith in its utility—in connection with science; but everything he says applies just as well to the business of hiring a private detective.

[O]ne does not want to let oneself be deceived because one assumes it is harmful, dangerous, disastrous to be deceived; in this sense science would be a long-range prudence, caution, utility, and to this one could justifiably object: How so? Is it really less harmful, dangerous, disastrous not to want to let oneself be deceived? What do you know in advance about the character of existence to be able to decide whether the greater advantage is on the side of the unconditionally distrustful or of the unconditionally trusting?[2]

Doesn't Nietzsche have a point? Can we really be so sure that what *they* say is true, when "they say the truth will set you free"—to quote Veronica at the moment she notes the irony of "looking for the truth in a maximum security prison," where Abel Koontz is held ("Like a Virgin")? The clients of Mars Investigations seem pretty confident that they're paying for something that will ultimately empower them in some way, but who's to say that they might not be better off being deceived?

Exposing the truth, like any other action, has consequences. So let's look at the explosive aftermaths of some of the truths that Veronica and others have uncovered in Neptune. Sometimes it's the destruction of promising careers, such as that of Geena Stafford. When Ms. Stafford, a Neptune High journalism teacher, publishes Veronica's exposé of the administration's knowledge of bomb threats directed at the school, she finds herself in conflict with then Vice-Principal Van Clemmons, who claims that her actions are at odds with the school's "very real duty to protect the student body"—a duty that he says trumps the "non-existent right to a free student press." When Ms. Stafford is fired, our sympathies are naturally with her; but, given the disruption that the story caused in the halls of Neptune High, it's possible that Clemmons had a point ("Weapons of Class Destruction"). A couple years later Veronica exposes the marijuana-growing room at the Theta Beta House on the Hearst College campus, causing sorority den mother and cancer patient Karen to lose her job, along with her health insurance—an outcome that Veronica deeply regrets ("My Big Fat Greek Rush Weekend").

Sometimes not just careers, but lives are put at risk when the truth is exposed. Consider Veronica's brush with death in the first season's finale, after uncovering the truth that Aaron Echolls murdered Lilly Kane, not to mention the bullet that Clarence Weidman plants in Aaron's skull at the conclusion of season 2. And what about Lilly herself? After all, it was her discovery and subsequent confiscation of the covertly recorded videotapes that provoked Aaron's outrage and directly resulted in her murder. Those dangerous tapes exposed a truth that Aaron did everything in his power to suppress. If *Veronica Mars* teaches us anything, it's that exposing the truth has consequences. If, like poor, doomed Lilly, you have "a secret"—"a good one!"—maybe the best course of action would be to keep it that way.

Consider also Keith's growing doubts, expressed at the end of "Return of the Kane," about the desirability of solving Lilly's murder. It's not because he thinks that solving the case would put anyone's life in danger, but because he no longer thinks that it will bring about all the good consequences that he hoped the truth would deliver. "I used to think that solving the case was the key to our happiness," he confesses to Veronica. "Solve the case and my reputation is restored. Solve the case and your mom comes home. Solve the case and you go back to being a normal teenager." But now he's become aware that his and Veronica's relentless pursuit of the truth about Lilly's death has begun to wreak havoc on their relationship. "What I believe in now is that we make the most out of what we have here and now," even if that means letting go of the desire for truth and choosing to remain in ignorance. Of course, once Veronica shows him the new evidence proving that Lilly's shoes were *not* in Abel Koontz's possession—contrary to the facts presented at the trial—Keith immediately becomes interested in the case again. Still, for a moment, he wonders whether the pursuit of truth is worth it.

But, if the pursuit of truth can be so destructive that even someone like Keith, who has such a stake in getting to the bottom of Lilly's murder, begins to question whether it's worth the trouble, we're forced to wonder whether knowing the truth is really such a great thing after all. With its constant reminder of the often painful consequences of the truth, *Veronica Mars* seems intent on making us question our faith in the value of the truth.

"Dad Always Says This Is the Job"

Not every doubt about the usefulness of truth in *Veronica Mars* is motivated by a father's love for his daughter. There are more sinister examples as well, such as when Principal Alan Moorehead attempts to instill in Veronica doubts about the value of truth in an effort to cover up his own misdeeds ("My Mother, the Fiend"). Moorehead deceives Veronica about her mother in order to conceal his abandonment of his own daughter—who was later adopted and grew up to be Trina Echolls—at the Neptune High prom, 25 years earlier. When Veronica discovers that her mother, Lianne Mars, was suspended from school for "spreading a false and malicious rumor about another student," she asks Mr. Moorehead, who was vice-principal when Lianne was a student, if he remembers what her mother was accused of saying. "Well, of course I don't, Veronica," he replies. "But even if I did, why would I want to repeat it?"

It turns out that Mr. Moorehead has a *very* good reason for not wanting to repeat that old rumor, for it concerns his affair with Trina's biological mother, Mary Mooney, who was then a student. But instead he dishonestly implies that his reticence is motivated by a desire to protect Veronica from having to confront unpleasant truths about her mother. Lying through his teeth, he says: "I'm sure your mom turned into a terrific person, but during the time she was here Lianne was rather vicious."

When Mr. Moorehead tries to convince Veronica that her mother was a fiend, his aim is to persuade her that she doesn't really want the truth after all, despite the motivations that brought her to him in the first place. He wants her to believe that the truth may not be useful for her after all, but could instead be harmful. In essence, he's asking her: "Do you *really* want to know?" But in this case the supposed danger of knowing the truth isn't that bad consequences will result from having the truth exposed, but rather that the knowledge itself will be painful to the knower, to such an extent that perhaps remaining in ignorance might be preferable.

Luckily Veronica doesn't fall for the ploy. But what if Lianne Mars *had been* "rather vicious" back in the day and Mr. Moorehead had been genuinely looking out for Veronica's best interests? Would his attempt to conceal those details from her have been acceptable? Are there things people are better off not knowing? To explore this question, we don't need to craft a thought experiment about the scandal-suppressing Mr. Moorehead. *Veronica Mars* is brimming with other examples.

Veronica may be willing to face hard truths about her mother, but things are very different when it comes to what a paternity test might tell her about her relationship with Keith. In "Drinking the Kool-Aid," one of the main plot arcs of the first season, undergoes an intriguing development when Veronica, who has been anxiously awaiting the results of her paternity test, has a surprising change of heart and decides instead to destroy those results before reading them. Rather than risk the emotional pain of discovering that Keith is *not* her father—a discovery that could jeopardize the most important relationship in her life—she sends the truth through the shredder and chooses ignorance instead.[3] It's hard to imagine an action more out of keeping with her character. "When have you ever not wanted to know anything?" Logan asks her in season 3 ("Of Vice and Men"). The answer is: when the truth may be too horrifying to bear. The possible harm that she anticipates from knowing the test results is so great that she deliberately chooses ignorance, albeit "with a side of gnawing doubt" ("Silence of the Lamb").[4]

A similar example of the great harm that the truth can cause is depicted in the experiences of Veronica's friend Cindy "Mac" Mackenzie when she has her suspicions confirmed that she's not in fact a Mackenzie ("Silence of the Lamb"). But, whereas Veronica's preemptive will to ignorance prevents her from actually feeling the pain that she can only imagine, Mac's pain and trauma become fully realized. It turns out that she was swapped soon after birth with the repugnant 09-er Madison Sinclair and sent home with the wrong family. Mac must now find a way to cope with the discovery that her years of enduring epithets like "freakball vegan" from Mrs. Natalie Mackenzie could have been spent in the vast and beautiful library of the Sinclair home—"Think she's even read five books in that library?" she wonders about Madison—were it not for some horrible mixup at the Neptune Memorial Hospital.

It would be hard to argue that Mac isn't in some very real sense harmed by this knowledge, though none of her material conditions change in the least. The only thing that changes is her understanding of who she is, but that abrupt shift in her self-perception causes her tremendous emotional pain. Her psychological torment is depicted with great poignancy in the final scene, when she and the mother she's never known mutually press their outstretched palms on Mrs. Ellen Sinclair's car window, only to then have Mrs. Sinclair drive off silently when Mac turns back to the false "parents" who have raised her.

Knowing the truth can sometimes be devastating. Would Mac have been better off not knowing? It's certainly possible. As Veronica reports, "Dad always says this is the job: Telling people stuff they might not want to know or might be better off not knowing" ("Silence of the Lamb"). Nietzsche entertains a similar possibility:

> The falseness of a judgment is for us not necessarily an objection to a judgment ... the question is to what extent it is life-promoting,

life-preserving, species-preserving, perhaps even species-cultivating. And we are fundamentally inclined to claim that the falsest judgments … are the most indispensable for us.[5]

According to Nietzsche, there may be times when a falsehood is indispensable for our well-being. Mac's experience leaves us wondering whether this might be one of those times. Has her life really been served by learning how things *could* have been? Perhaps we're all better off living in a world of what Nietzsche calls "simplification and falsification," filtering out anything that hinders our enjoyment of life.[6] Or, as Veronica suggests after exposing the criminal domestic troubles of her neighbor Sarah Williams, perhaps there "are some things better left buried" ("The Girl Next Door").

Veronica the *Versucher*

But if the truth isn't always useful, if indeed it can be harmful, painful, and even psychologically devastating, why do we so often persist in pursuing the truth about things? Keith might say that he does it because that's "the job." For scientists and philosophers (such as the other contributors to this volume), it could also be a job and a paycheck. But what draws many of us to these truth-seeking professions, or rather vocations, seems to be a conviction that the value of the truth isn't reducible to the paycheck we get. Rather the truth strikes many of us as something good in itself, even unconditionally good. It's not just a means to an end, but something inherently edifying and uplifting to know. If this is what we believe, then Nietzsche argues that our "faith in science … must have originated *in spite of* the fact that the disutility and dangerousness of 'the will to truth' or 'truth at any price' is proved to it constantly." It must rest upon "a *metaphysical faith*," which Nietzsche finds highly questionable, "that truth is divine … But what if this were to become more and more difficult to believe, if nothing more were to turn out to be divine except error, blindness, the lie?"[7]

These are challenging questions. What should we do once we realize that the unconditional will to truth is based on a faith that lacks any demonstrable certainty that the truth is desirable? And if people are often better off not knowing the truth—if, in the words of the radio signoff used by Marcos Oliveres (aka Cap'n Krunk), "Truth hurts; I'm out!" ("Ahoy Mateys")—should we just suppress or relinquish our desire for the truth?[8] Not necessarily, at least not according to Nietzsche. In his writings, Nietzsche repeatedly poses the question of the value of truth, awakening in his readers a curiosity about whether truth really is valuable for life after all. In a similar way, *Veronica Mars* repeatedly poses the question of the value of truth, offering viewers many opportunities to appreciate how costly and dangerous the pursuit of the truth can be. But, by forcing us to ask those questions, both Nietzsche and *Veronica Mars* kindle in us the very love of truth that they call into question. For, every time we ask about the value of truth, every time we ponder whether the truth is worth the cost and we exert our minds to try to find it out, we are acting like sleuths and philosophers who can no more turn away from a good mystery or conundrum than Dick Casablancas could pass up a hot co-ed with low self-esteem. If the truth is dangerous, well, some of us must love living close to the edge.

In *Beyond Good and Evil*, Nietzsche speaks of "a new species of philosophers" that he believes is coming up, christening them with a name that, he says, "is not free of danger."[9] The name he risks is *Versucher*—which we could translate as attempters, tempters, experimenters, or maybe even risk-takers. In proposing this name, Nietzsche seems to be deliberately luring us to enter the risky business of experimentation. He's daring us to ask the most difficult questions, even though we may suspect that the answers could be unsettling, painful, and even injurious. We can't always know whether the knowledge we seek is good for us, but we can admire the courage and fortitude of the intrepid truth-seeking sleuth or philosopher, the *Versucher*, pursuing her investigations wherever they might lead and regardless of their cost.

Are you willing to take the risk?

Acknowledgment

I am grateful to George Dunn for the very insightful comments and suggestions he made on an earlier draft of this chapter.

Notes

1. Friedrich Nietzsche, *Beyond Good and Evil*, trans. Walter Kaufmann (New York: Vintage Books, 1966), 9.
2. Friedrich Nietzsche, *The Gay Science*, trans. Josefine Nauckhoff (New York: Cambridge University Press, 2001), 200.
3. In a characteristically brilliantly written episode, the minor plot of Veronica's paternity is contrasted with happenings at the Moon Calf Collective, an organization assumed throughout the episode to be a cult. The expectation throughout "Drinking the Kool-Aid" is that Veronica is going to uncover the weird happenings at the Collective and to show how its members have all drunk the "Kool-Aid," but it turns out that none of them actually has. The episode closes with Veronica's exercise in literally shredding the truth and thereby (in a sense) drinking the Kool-Aid herself. The regularity with which *Veronica Mars* forces us to question the value of the truth makes it an ideal vehicle to discuss Nietzsche's thoughts on the subject.
4. For more on Veronica's attitude toward the value of truth, see Chapter 5 in this volume, by Daniel Wack.
5. Nietzsche, *Beyond Good and Evil*, 11–12.
6. Ibid., 35.
7. Nietzsche, *The Gay Science*, 201.

8. This possibility is easier to entertain than you might imagine. For instance, it's the conclusion drawn by the philosopher Richard Rorty, who writes: "It was Nietzsche who first explicitly suggested that we drop the whole idea of 'knowing the truth.'" Richard Rorty, *Contingency, Irony, and Solidarity* (New York: Cambridge University Press, 1989), 27.

9. Nietzsche, *Beyond Good and Evil*, 52.

"Have You Ever Heard of Occam's Razor?"

Veronica's Use of Inductive Reasoning

Andrew Zimmerman Jones

Veronica Mars's life would be a lot easier—though less interesting—if she didn't live in a world where the truth was hidden behind layers of obscurity. Thankfully, she's skilled at—and even obsessed with—peeling back those layers to reveal the underlying truth. In her world, as in ours, the easy answers are not always the correct ones.

The master detective and the classical philosopher both regard logic as a driving force in the search for truth. The truth they seek is usually very different, of course. While the philosopher is typically concerned with general arguments that apply across a wide range of well-defined cases, Veronica is usually looking for the explanation behind some specific situation, such as a murder or someone's disappearance, which is often not nearly as well defined as she would like.

Occam's Razor Defeats "Sinister Forces"

When Hearst College student Billy "Sully" Sullivan goes missing, his girlfriend Meryl asks Veronica to help track him down. Veronica

Veronica Mars and Philosophy: Investigating the Mysteries of Life (Which is a Bitch Until You Die), First Edition. Edited by George A. Dunn.
© 2014 John Wiley & Sons, Inc. Published 2014 by Wiley Blackwell.

is skeptical about the case, since she doesn't believe there's any real mystery to be solved. What's so mysterious about a guy standing up his girlfriend? Yet Meryl is certain that Sully wouldn't have abandoned their planned weekend together of his own accord. "I called all the hospitals," she says. "I talked to his professors and no one's seen or heard from him." And then she offers her own fanciful hypothesis about what might have happened:

> Look, I was just thinking. Sully told me that in his physics class, they're working with lasers. So what if Sully accidentally discovered some new technology, you know, like some kind of laser cannon that could assassinate people from space or something? He could be running from, I don't know, sinister forces! ("Of Vice and Men")

Veronica waves off Meryl's speculation that Sully is on the lam from sinister forces. But how can we justify rejecting it out of hand, since it is at least *possible* that this sequence of events really happened?

Veronica's response to Meryl's space laser speculation neatly sums up why we feel justified in rejecting it without even needing to question Sully's physics professor and classmates about possible space lasers:

VERONICA	Have you ever heard of Occam's razor, Meryl?
MERYL	Is it a space laser? Has it already been invented?
VERONICA	No, it's a theory. Basically, the theory states that when given a set of possible explanations for a phenomenon, we should embrace the least complicated. So, I guess I'm saying that if, on the one hand, you have Sully inventing a space laser and, on the other, maybe he wants to break up but is taking the coward's way out … ("Of Vice and Men")

Developed by the medieval philosopher William of Ockham (1287–1347), Occam's razor is neither a space laser nor, strictly speaking, a theory, though Veronica's explanation is otherwise right on the mark. A *theory* offers a comprehensive explanation of some set of phenomena, for example, the theory of evolution in biology or atomic theory in physics. By contrast, Occam's razor is a principle, one that helps us to eliminate unlikely explanations, specifically those that depend on unnecessary assumptions. The name "razor" refers to how this principle *shaves* those assumptions away. Care must be taken, however, not to shave any assumption away prematurely, as Veronica herself learns when she discovers what actually happened to Sully.

Often referred to as "the principle of parsimony" or "the principle of simplicity," Occam's razor has been summed up in many ways over the centuries. Some examples are:

- Plurality should not be posited without necessity.
- It is futile to do with more things that which can be done with fewer.
- "Whenever possible, substitute constructions out of known entities for inferences to unknown entities": Bertrand Russell (1872–1970).
- "Everything should be made as simple as possible, but no simpler": attributed to Albert Einstein (1879–1955).

Whatever way you word it, the key element of Occam's razor is *favoring simplicity over complexity*. Simplicity is always to be preferred in an explanation, except when adding complexity offers a more detailed or comprehensive explanation.[1] Occam's razor is a "heuristic tool," which is a fancy way of saying that it's not guaranteed always to work, but it does often help when solving problems.

Occam's Razor Solves the Case
of the Missing Pick-up

While investigating Gia Goodman's stalker, Veronica discovers a video showing the person who filmed the footage sent to Gia. There he is, wearing a Neptune high school letterman jacket and holding a camera. Watching the video, Veronica found another clue:

VERONICA   There, see, the red truck. It's gone and so is he. It must be his.

GIA   Snap!

VERONICA   So now we just have to find a varsity letterman who drives a red pick-up and we've got our stalker. ("Look Who's Stalking")

Though Veronica doesn't invoke Occam's razor by name this time, her line of reasoning offers a good example of the razor at work. Nothing demands that the disappearances of the pick-up truck and of the jacket wearer must be linked just because they occurred at the same time. It's quite possible that the owner of the truck just happened to drive off at the same time that the stalker left. However, Occam's razor suggests that we look at these explanations side by side and consider which is the most parsimonious or the simplest:

1   The stalker drove off in the pick-up truck.
2   Someone else drove off in the pick-up truck at the same time the stalker left.

Both of these explanations completely match the evidence at Veronica's disposal, but the second requires a hypothetical extra person. It "unnecessarily posits a plurality," "does with more things what could be done with fewer," and "constructs with references to unknown entities rather than known entities." In short, it's unnecessarily complex.

Simply put, the extra person in the second explanation isn't needed to account for the evidence, so Occam's razor suggests that we should dispense with him and go with the simpler explanation, as Veronica intuitively understands. And indeed, Occam's razor leads her to the right culprit: Tommy "Lucky" Dohanic.

But there are times when the simplest explanation can lead you astray.

Razors, Brooms, and Bear Claws

When Abel Koontz confessed to the murder of Lilly Kane, there were two possible ways to make sense of his confession:

1   Abel Koontz's confession is true. He murdered Lilly Kane.
2   Abel Koontz's confession is false. Someone else murdered Lilly Kane.

In this case, the first option is clearly the more parsimonious: there's a confessor and a murderer—and they're the same person. The second option means that you have not only to figure out why Abel Koontz would give a false confession, but also to search for another murderer. Why substitute an "unknown entity" when you already have one that's "known"? Yet Keith Mars rejects the simpler explanation and goes after Jake Kane, a move that ends up costing Keith his job as sheriff ("Pilot"). Is Keith ignorant of Occam's razor?

Not necessarily. Recall that Occam's razor says that we should seek the simplest possible explanation that accounts for all of the known facts. But if our explanation is so simple that there are facts it can't explain, that won't cut it either. That only turns Occam's razor into an excuse for Sheriff Don Lamb to stop working on a case whenever he wants to take a break to eat another bear claw!

Lamb's insouciance is an example of what molecular biologist Sidney Brenner has dubbed Occam's broom, "the process in which inconvenient facts are whisked under the rug by intellectually dishonest champions of one theory or another."[2] Note, though, that, while this whisking away of inconvenient facts may be intellectually dishonest, its dishonesty isn't necessarily conscious. It might just reflect an unconscious mental bias. Lamb could genuinely believe that Abel Koontz is guilty and that Keith's suspicion of Jake Kane is unjustified. What makes the use of Occam's broom particularly problematic is that it often takes an expert to recognize when the whisking is unjustified.

Being such an expert, Keith knows that something isn't right about Koontz's confession: there are facts surrounding the murder that it doesn't explain. For example, Keith knows that the Kanes took time to do laundry on the evening of the murder, that Jake Kane also called Clarence Wiedman that night, and that Lilly's core body temperature didn't match the alleged time of death ("Kanes and Abel's"). Veronica later discovers that the clothes found in Koontz's house had been in Lilly's bedroom after the murder ("Return of the Kane"). When she learns that Koontz is dying of cancer and that his daughter is receiving substantial payments from the Kanes, it becomes more and more necessary to "posit some plurality" to explain all this new evidence ("Betty and Veronica")—and that's exactly what Keith and Veronica's expertise allows them to do.

"Life's a Bitch, then You Die" — Probably!

Occam's razor (and Occam's broom) aside, someone can be forgiven for assuming that a person who confesses to a crime is probably the person who committed it. You don't need to be as incurious as Sheriff Lamb to recognize that the probability of a person falsely confessing to a murder is pretty low. But how do we arrive at that conclusion? Through a process known to philosophers as inductive reasoning. Recognized as far back at Aristotle (384–322 BCE), typically "an induction argues 'from particulars to universal,' that is, infers a general claim from a number of its instances."[3] Thus, if, in all the cases we know about, innocent people very rarely voluntarily confess to murder, then we can apply inductive reasoning to these "particulars" and infer the "general" conclusion that there's a high probability that anyone who confesses to murder is guilty of it.[4]

Inductive reasoning is contrasted with deductive reasoning, which typically begins from a general statement of principle ("Anyone who confesses to murder is probably guilty") and moves to a more specific conclusion ("Abel Koontz is probably guilty"). One classic example of deductive argument begins from the general principle "All human beings are mortal" and ends with the conclusion that a specific man, the Greek philosopher Socrates (429–399 BCE), is mortal. If the initial statement "All human beings are mortal" is true, then the conclusion *must* also be true. But how do we discover the truth of this general statement in the first place? According to Aristotle, we derive general principles through inductive reasoning, which gives induction a sort of primacy in our logical toolkit.[5]

The inductive argument that would lead us to conclude that all human beings are mortal might run something like this:

1   Lilly Kane is mortal.
2   Kendall Casablancas is mortal.
3   Cassidy Casablancas is mortal.
4   Meg Manning is mortal.
5   Dean Cyrus O'Dell is mortal.
6   Sheriff Don Lamb is mortal.
7   Countless other human beings, both in and outside of Neptune, are mortal.
Therefore,
8   All human beings are mortal (probably).

But notice the qualifier "probably," which is there to remind us that this inductive argument can't give us absolute certainty, no matter how many examples we pile up (and there are *plenty* more examples that we could draw from the show—Neptune's mortality rate rivals that of Sunnydale). There's always the possibility that new evidence could force us to revise our conclusion, say, if immortal human beings showed up in Neptune (maybe in a *Veronica/Buffy* crossover film).

Sheriff Lamb's belief in Koontz's guilt relies on the universal principle that a person who voluntarily confesses to a crime is almost certainly guilty of that crime, though Lamb is undoubtedly aware that there are exceptions to this rule. He refuses to spend time and resources investigating the possibility that someone else is the killer *not* because he's absolutely certain that every single person who confesses is guilty of the crime. Even Lamb isn't that arrogant (we hope)! Rather, he uses Occam's broom to dismiss all the other evidence that points away from Koontz. He's decided in advance that following up on that evidence isn't worth his effort. After all, there are bear claws to be eaten…

Probability, Cologne, and Hair Clippers

When Veronica learns that she's contracted chlamydia, her doctor asks: "Have you been sexually active at all within the last year or two?" Veronica replies: "We were, you know, safe, and the guy, there's no way he …" Her expression of disbelief prompts her doctor to remind her: "You think that, but you never know" ("Look Who's Stalking"). He may not be doing so intentionally, but Veronica's doctor is actually pointing out one of the central problems of inductive reasoning: We think we know things, but we never really do, at least not with certainty. So, if some degree of probability is the best we can hope for when reasoning about events in the world, how do we go about judging what's more or less probable?

Sheriff Lamb is initially skeptical when Veronica tells him that she's found someone who not only owns hair clippers, a tool used by the Hearst rapist, but also wears the same cologne as the rapist ("Hi, Infidelity"). But Lamb's interest is piqued once he learns that Veronica is talking about Mercer Hayes, for it turns out that the cashbox stolen from Mercer's underground casino ("President Evil") contained two vials of the date-rape drug gamma-hydroxybutyric acid (GHB), which was used by the rapist on his victims. In an odd twist, Logan asks Veronica to prove Mercer's innocence, despite her being the one who first drew attention to Mercer as a suspect. During a jailhouse visit, she and Mercer discuss the evidence against him:

> MERCER   The sheriff seemed awfully interested in my cologne. *GQ* had a sample of it in the Back to School issue, so I hardly think that's some huge clue. Now, do you think I'm the only guy at Hearst who owns clippers and subscribes to *Gentleman's Quarterly*?
>
> VERONICA   And keeps a stockpile of GHB handy … from what I hear. ("Of Vice and Men")

At this point there are the three pieces of evidence incriminating Mercer: the clippers, the cologne, and the GHB. But Mercer is right to note that there could be other male students at Hearst with the same cologne and a set of hair clippers, so this evidence is highly circumstantial. The GHB is much more damaging; but, given that GHB seems to flow like water through the Neptune social scene, even it isn't conclusive. There's plenty of room for reasonable doubt, even though it might not seem so at first blush.

If the evidence seems to leave little room for doubt, this may be because we have difficulty recognizing the difference between two sorts of probability. Consider the following two statements:

1 The probability is high that the rapist is someone who owns clippers, a certain cologne, and GHB.
2 The probability is high that someone (like Mercer) who owns clippers, a certain cologne, and GHB is the rapist.

Statement 1 is true. There's a close to 100 percent probability that the rapist owns those three things. Statement 2, on the other hand, may not be true at all, because there could be any number of men other than the rapist who own those three things. Even if we assume that there are only five men on campus who own them, that still yields only a 20 percent chance that Mercer is the rapist. That falls far short of proof, no matter how convincing the evidence may otherwise look and feel.

This kind of difference is often overlooked, perhaps even intentionally, in public debates on a variety of issues. Consider the impact in racial and social tensions that can result from confusing these two statements:

1   The probability is high that a given PCH-er commits crimes.
2   The probability is high that a given crime was committed by a PCH-er.

Again, we have a situation where the first statement may be true, without its truth necessarily making the second statement true. After all, not all crimes in Neptune are committed by PCH-ers. Many are committed by Fitzpatricks and Casablancas!

But let's get back to the rape case. Veronica sets out to falsify the hypothesis that Mercer is the rapist, and apparently she succeeds when she uncovers evidence that he was live on the radio during two of the rapes. Moreover, Veronica is herself drugged with GHB and attacked in the Hearst parking garage while Mercer is still in police custody ("Of Vice and Men"). Quite reasonably, this new evidence causes her to revise her estimation of the likelihood that Mercer is the rapist.

Of course, she arrives at this new conclusion by way of a huge assumption that turns out to be incorrect: the assumption that there's a single rapist. In fact there are two rapists working as a team, which is how some abductions could occur while Mercer was broadcasting his radio show. While hiding in the closet of Mercer's accomplice Moe Slater, Veronica stumbles upon the most damning piece of physical evidence yet: the shaved hair trophies from the rape victims ("Spit & Eggs"). Consider the probability of the following statement:

Someone who keeps trophies from rape victims is a rapist.

One doesn't need to intern with the FBI or to have a degree in criminal psychology to know that there's a strong likelihood of that statement's being true. Though we never find out for sure what happens to Mercer and Moe, we can only hope that their jury does a better job of evaluating evidence than Aaron Echolls's jury did.

"I Wouldn't Have Believed It Either"

Despite Veronica's expertise in the use of Occam's razor and avoidance of Occam's broom, there are occasions when Veronica is wrong, not just because she doesn't have all the facts, but because she's the victim of her own cognitive biases. Her brain leads her astray, causing her to apply reasoning that is clearly flawed.

Recall her conversation with Meryl, in which she contrasted two hypotheses to account for Sully's disappearance: "on the one hand, you have Sully inventing a space laser and, on the other, maybe he wants to break up but is taking the coward's way out" ("Of Vice and Men"). This is a perfect example of the logical fallacy known as a "false dilemma," in which two options are presented as if they were the only ones. Of these two options, "he wants to break up" is clearly the better choice, but other possibilities are ignored, such as "Sully went surfing and suffered an amnesia-inducing head wound." And it's that ignored possibility that turns out to be the true explanation.

This episode is a treasure trove of logical fallacies, for reasons that are easy to see: the episode is built around Veronica's frustration and anxiety over her relationship with Logan, Keith's adulterous relationship with Harmony Chase, and Professor Hank Landry's apparent attempt to buy Veronica's silence with an internship. These emotional factors drive her toward not only the simplest, but also the most tawdry explanation of Sully's disappearance. "You have a fight and then he's not around when you fly in," she says, reviewing the evidence for Meryl. "That doesn't make you the least bit suspicious?" But Meryl says that it doesn't.

Veronica believes that Meryl is dangerously naïve, but the truth is that Veronica may be committing yet another logical fallacy: the fallacy of attributing a "false cause," where one event (Meryl's fight with Sully) is taken as the cause of another (Sully's disappearance) simply because it preceded the other in time. Of course, it's *possible* that after a fight a miffed boyfriend might want to break up but makes himself scarce instead, in order to avoid a confrontation. However, we'd need to know much more about Sully before we could conclude that this is the best explanation. If Meryl doesn't jump to this hasty conclusion, it's because she has inside knowledge that Veronica lacks. She's able to recognize her "knock-down, drag-out" with Sully over the phone as "just the long-distance stuff getting to us" rather than as the prelude to a breakup. "I know what it looked like," she tells Veronica after Sully is found, conceding that Veronica's conclusion wasn't entirely unreasonable. "If I hadn't been in love before, I wouldn't have believed it either." What Meryl doesn't realize is that Veronica's recent experience in love is one of the things that have been coloring her reasoning through this whole ordeal.

Veronica's emotional state in the episode is most evident when she commits what I regard as the worst of all logical fallacies: the "*ad hominem* attack"—ignoring the merits of the other person's argument completely, refusing even to engage with the facts, and attacking the person instead. Veronica succumbs to this fallacy when she and Meryl confront Sully's "study buddy" Scarlett in the cafeteria. Having decided in advance to dismiss anything that the suspiciously well-dressed girl has to say, Veronica turns to Meryl and declares: "Scarlett here has either stolen your boyfriend or she wants to. That's just the way it is. You can choose to be a patsy or you can choose not to be."

This "patsy/not a patsy" alternative could be seen as another false dilemma. Moreover, Veronica poses it in a way that entangles her in yet another logical fallacy, known as "appeal to emotion." In essence, Veronica is saying to Meryl: "If you don't accept my explanation of Sully's disappearance, you're a *patsy*. You don't want to be a *patsy*, do you?" Instead of appealing to reason and evidence, Veronica tries to persuade Meryl by manipulating her emotions. In sum, this episode illustrates several of the logical fallacies that can sidetrack the reasoning of otherwise excellent thinkers (and Veronica is undoubtedly one of the best), as well as the ways in which emotions can sometimes hobble our ability to think logically.

When Life Gives You Chlamydia

Let's wrap this up with one last example that highlights both the limitations of inductive reasoning and Veronica's use of Occam's razor. In "Leave It to Beaver" Veronica constructs an account of what happened to her the night she lost her virginity. She learns that it was Duncan Kane who crawled into bed with her and that the encounter, while still not entirely consensual, wasn't exactly what she had originally believed it to be. Occam's razor suggests that there's no reason for her to believe that there's anything more to the story, since all the known facts are explained—or at least the facts she knew at the time.

But new facts emerge when she's later diagnosed with chlamydia. She knows she couldn't have gotten it from Duncan, though he's the only person with whom she *knows* she had sex ("Look Who's Stalking"). When she discovers that her ailment is shared by Mayor Woody Goodman, who had sexually abused boys on the Little League team he coached, and when she subsequently learns that Cassidy "Beaver" Casablancas was a member of that team, she infers that he was the most likely source of her infection and that he had lied when he denied having touched her that night. Veronica's previous conclusion that she hadn't been raped must now give way to a new conclusion, which is based on new evidence.

All this is a brutal lesson in how tenuous our grasp on truth is. Veronica has learned that nothing is certain and that she must be skeptical about everything. Certainty is a sucker's bet. And if there's one thing Veronica Mars is *not*, that's a sucker.

Notes

1. For more on the principle that simpler explanations are better, see Chapter 15 in this volume, by Daniel A. Wilkenfeld.
2. Daniel C. Dennett, *Intuition Pumps and Other Tools for Thinking* (New York: W. W. Norton, 2013), 40.
3. Robin Smith, "Logic," in Jonathan Barnes, ed., *The Cambridge Companion to Aristotle* (Cambridge: Cambridge University Press, 1995), 30.
4. Of course, we're not concerned here with coerced confessions, where there's a much higher probability that the accused is innocent. But Abel Koontz's confession appears to have been entirely voluntary.
5. Aristotle, *Posterior Analytics*, book 2, ch. 19, in Richard McKeon, ed., *The Basic Works of Aristotle* (New York: Modern Library, 1941), 185–186.

15

"Not Pictured"
What Veronica Knew but Didn't See

Daniel A. Wilkenfeld

There's so much more to being a detective than just seeing the clues right in front of your eyes. What makes a detective great is that she can figure out the truth she's *not* seeing—the hidden explanation behind an otherwise scattered array of facts and appearances. She can puzzle through the observed facts to get at the hidden truth. That's where Veronica Mars excels, and that's what makes her special. Veronica is, of course, no stranger to fieldwork. She has no trouble breaking into a house, and she even mocks Duncan Kane ("Nobody Puts Baby in a Corner") and later Tim Foyle ("Papa's Cabin") for their romanticized notion of what it takes to get actual detecting done. But, to my mind, all the fieldwork in the world doesn't add up to a great detective. Being a detective is more than just being a well-trained bloodhound that can pick up a scent—it's about being able to think, reason, and make good inferences.

Veronica Mars and Philosophy: Investigating the Mysteries of Life (Which is a Bitch Until You Die), First Edition. Edited by George A. Dunn.
© 2014 John Wiley & Sons, Inc. Published 2014 by Wiley Blackwell.

Veronica's Magic Trick

Sometimes Veronica can be a great detective without even leaving a room. In "One Angry Veronica" she spends pretty much the entire episode locked in a juryroom. Interestingly, she only gets one "new" piece of information in the whole episode: that an allegedly fence-jumping pimp in fact had a serious knee problem. All the other relevant facts are presented to the jury during the trial, which we don't get to see. The real detective work goes on in the juryroom.

What detecting does Veronica do from inside the juryroom? The facts, as presented, are as follows. After a day of work at the car wash, a young Latina ends up in a hotel room with a pair of 09-ers. Two shots are fired into the ceiling and she is later found beaten. Twelve minutes after the shots, a young black man flees the scene, jumping a six-foot fence. No gun is ever found, though a man who claims to be the woman's pimp later confesses to the beating. Despite the alleged pimp's confession, the two 09-ers are now on trial, accused of having beaten the woman.

At first Veronica believes the 09-ers' story that the woman was a prostitute whose pimp fired the shots before beating her up. However, she, along with her fellow jurors, comes to realize that not all of the facts add up to form a coherent picture. There are several things that go unexplained on the 09-ers' account:

1   Their story that the victim was a prostitute doesn't explain why she worked a full day at the car wash.
2   Their story doesn't account for the 12-minute delay between the shots' being fired and the alleged pimp's fleeing the scene.
3   Their story leaves unexplained why the "pimp" would turn himself in.

Thinking about how to explain these facts, Veronica constructs a new narrative that, if accurate, would account for everything that everyone already knows. She concludes that the 09-ers did in fact beat the girl, that she fired her own gun into the air, and that she had a friend remove the illegal firearm. The 09-ers then hired someone to pretend to be her pimp and take the rap for the crime.

What Veronica did has the air of a magic trick: she started with one bunch of facts, applied some thought to them, and somehow ended up with a brand new view of an event that she didn't actually see herself. She thought of a story that would account for all the facts and concluded that this story must be what actually happened.

The construction of a narrative from otherwise disparate facts is at the heart of most of the important revelations in the series. In the climactic moments of the first and second seasons (though, sadly, not in the third), the camera rushes toward Veronica's face as she puts together the pieces of a year-long mystery to form one coherent, explanatory story. We're left with the impression that she has somehow "seen" the answer, in a remarkable moment of intuition. But what has she "seen"? And how has she "seen" it? And, perhaps most importantly, why should she—or anyone—trust these things that she's merely "seen" in her mind?

Leave It to Beaver

Philosophers have long been interested in the way in which some beliefs support others. *Inference* is the word used by philosophers for the process by which we start from old beliefs and make our way to new ones on their basis.

The ideal case is called a *deductive inference*, in which the truth of our conclusion is guaranteed so long as the beliefs we started with are also true. Let's say that Veronica knows that Eli "Weevil" Navarro, Duncan Kane, Logan Echolls, Sean Friedrich, or Conner Larkin stole the money. Let's also say that she knows that Weevil didn't do it, Duncan didn't do it, Logan didn't do it, and Conner didn't do it. She can then be sure that Sean took the money ("An Echolls Family Christmas"). The example might seem somewhat trivial, and that's exactly the problem with deductive inferences: they don't usually lead to interesting conclusions. Even when the conclusion is interesting, it was always in some sense already contained in the original information, waiting to be teased out. Anyone who understood all the basic facts could easily infer that Sean stole the money and be absolutely certain of that conclusion. Deductive inferences don't go beyond the given facts in the same way Veronica's magic trick in the juryroom seems to.

There is, though, another class of inferences, in which we do go beyond the data in front of us to reach new beliefs. They're called *inductive inferences*. But, even when such inferences take us beyond the given facts, we still want our conclusions to be as likely as possible, even if they can never be 100 percent certain. If we always waited around for 100 percent certainty before saying or doing anything, almost nothing would ever get said or done. When Veronica realizes that a possibly drugged girl is missing from the Pi Sig party, she can't be 100 percent sure that the Hearst rapist has chosen his next victim, but it would have been grossly irresponsible of her not to act quickly ("Spit & Eggs"). Still, even in the absence of certainty, we need to try to make our inductive inferences as reasonable as possible.

One way to think about the importance of inductive inferences is by focussing on one of Veronica's most impressive feats of reasoning—her solving of the Neptune High bus crash. Putting together the story behind the crash takes Veronica an entire season. It involves some gathering of raw data, but it mostly requires an uncanny knack for seeing the truth behind the known facts.

To begin with, Veronica knows that a bus carrying Neptune High students, which the 09-ers had abandoned for a private ride as a result of an inexplicable foul odor, went over a cliff ("Normal Is the Watchword"). She soon uncovers a voice mail left by a student on the bus, on which an explosion can be heard before the bus goes over the edge ("Blast from the Past). She learns of a dead rat taped to the bottom of a seat in the recovered bus ("My Mother the Fiend"). Eventually, she learns that several students on the bus had been molested by Mayor Woody Goodman and were planning to come forward with their story ("Happy Go Lucky"). Veronica also draws on facts that seemingly have no connection with the original puzzle, such as Cassidy "Beaver" Cassablancas's uncanny business savvy (he has the best performance in the Future Business Leaders of America club) and her own chlamydia infection ("Look Who's Stalking").

What sort of inference does Veronica draw when she determines that Beaver is responsible for the crash? Her thought process looks something like this:

1   There's a bunch of facts she's sure of—that there was an explosion on the bus, that someone left a rat on it, that someone was able to trick the PCH-ers into taking out explosives-expert David "Curly" Moran, and that she somehow got chlamydia. On the surface these facts have no direct connection to each other, but they all prove to be important pieces in the story she reconstructs.

2   She learns that Beaver was one of Woody's victims and hence would have had a motive to see people on the bus silenced ("Not Pictured"). She also utilizes seemingly irrelevant background information—that Beaver was alone with her at Shelly Pomeroy's party ("A Trip to the Dentist") and that he had produced an amateur movie that required a pyrotechnics consultation ("Mars vs Mars")—to construct an explanation of the bus crash that ties together many different threads into one elegant story.

3   She concludes that, if Beaver were a killer (and therefore also probably not above rape), that would provide one really good *explanation* for the crash. It would also explain Curly

Moran's involvement (he knew Beaver), the presence of the dead rat on the bus (it was used to get Beaver and his closest associates off the bus), and even the seemingly unconnected fact of Veronica's own sexually transmitted disease (STD).

4   She *infers* that Beaver is probably a killer.

Her conclusion that Beaver is a killer is supported by the fact that his guilt would make a really nice explanation of the original phenomenon under investigation. We'll say a bit more in the next section about what makes it so nice, but the most important element is that a wide array of seemingly diverse facts are explained in one simple hypothesis.

We thus call this an *inference to the best explanation*; and, because Beaver's guilt would be such a good explanation, she infers that he must truly be guilty. It's a special kind of inductive inference, but what exactly makes it work?

"That Would Explain the Absence of Balloon Animals"

Peter Lipton (1954–2007) is the philosopher who has done the most to set out how such inferences work.[1] He notes that, on one way of talking, something counts as an explanation only if it is true. But when we say that people try to infer the *best* explanation, we can't just mean that they try to infer the *true* one. After all, if we already knew which explanation was true, we wouldn't have to do any inferring in the first place. We can't use truth as a criterion for determining which explanation is best, because we don't know what's most likely to be true until we're done making our inference. Thus the way inferences to the best explanation work is this: we identify some *other* features of explanations that make them good, and then we assume that those other features also make the explanations likely to be true.

But this raises two questions that should be of concern not just to someone like Veronica, who makes her living from inferences to the best explanation, but to the rest of us as well, since we all rely on inference to the best explanation, perhaps more than we realize. First, what makes an explanation better? And, perhaps more importantly, why do we think that better explanations are more likely to be true? We know that such inferences don't guarantee truth in the way a deductive inference would. Looking for a good explanation of why a stolen credit card was used to pay for a hotel room with Logan's then girlfriend Caitlin Ford, Veronica wrongly infers that Logan stole the credit card ("Credit Where Credit's Due"). Given that inferences to the best explanation are fallible, what reason do we have to think that they would be likely to get us any closer to the truth at all?

Let's begin with the question of what it is that makes an explanation better or best. What would be some measures of the goodness of an explanation?[2] One measure is how broad the explanation is, or how many different things it explains. Philosophers sometimes call this property *consilience*. If Veronica can wrap up a whole season's worth of mysteries in a single hypothesis, that's an *extremely* satisfying explanation. ("Beaver is a killer" gets bonus points not only for wrapping up the mysteries of season 2, but for providing a new solution to the mystery of Veronica's rape that had appeared settled at the end of season 1.)

Consilience is related to another desirable feature of explanations: *simplicity*. In general we prefer explanations that account for more with less. That we prefer simpler explanations is so commonplace that we generally don't even notice it. When Meryl suggests that perhaps her missing boyfriend invented some sort of new weapon and is on the run from "sinister forces," Veronica rejects the idea out of hand for its flagrant violation of Occam's razor ("Of Vice and Men")—the principle that, all else being equal, the simplest explanation is the best.[3] A hypothesis that involves the invention of secret death rays is rightly rejected as *needlessly* complicated. (Again, we see that these rules of thumb for evaluating explanations are imperfect guides to truth, for the real explanation of the mystery of the missing boyfriend proves to be much more complex than Veronica's preferred "simple" explanation, which is that Meryl's boyfriend had simply dumped her and run off.)

Another good feature of an explanation is *completeness*. When attempting to identify the Hearst rapist, it is not really *necessary* for Veronica to figure out *how* the victims were rendered unconscious; all that really matters is that they were. However, when we know that they were given drugged tea by their supposed "safe ride," the explanation somehow feels more satisfying and hence appears to be better. To the extent that those feelings are a reliable guide, a more complete explanation will be better than a less complete one. This feature is slightly different from consilience, which gains points for explaining a broader array of facts (or making them converge). By contrast, the criterion of completeness rates an explanation as superior if it accounts for a narrower set of facts in greater detail.

We might note that the Hearst rapist explanation loses some points with respect to consilience, as it never really accounts for the rape of Nancy Cooper, which occurred while Mercer Hayes was with Logan in Mexico. This doesn't prove that the explanation is false, though, since Nancy's rape could have an independent explanation. It could have been another rape faked by the members of Lillith House; or Mercer's accomplice, Moe Sater, could have gone into business for himself.

Why Would Anyone Assume that "Normal" Is the Watchword?

We could list more desirable features of explanations, but hopefully by now the gist is clear enough: we prefer explanations that hang together and tell a more complete story with minimal extraneous assumptions. Here, then, is the big question: While such explanations might make for better stories, why do we think they are any more likely to be true? Why do we think that our preference for certain types of stories corresponds to the way the world is actually set up? Maybe "better" explanations are really just those that play to our preexisting psychological biases.

Looking at our desirable features one by one, we can question whether there's any reason to suppose that explanations with that feature would be more likely to be true. Veronica infers that Beaver is the killer because that explanation would be consilient—it would explain a lot of seemingly diverse facts. But why assume that different types of facts are likely to share a single explanation? Maybe the real causal structure of the universe is complicated, so that sometimes simple explanations explain diverse facts, but sometimes even simple facts require complicated explanations. Or maybe we live in a complex universe where simple explanations are always less likely to be true. Things look even worse for completeness. Why should a more detailed story be more likely to be true? Suppose Veronica never figured out how the victims of the Hearst rapist were rendered unconscious—it would still have been a fact that they were.

You might think that there's an obvious answer to all these concerns—look at how well inference to the best explanation has worked in real life! How could it not be a good procedure? Veronica does, after all, have an incredible track record of being right, at least when the issue doesn't involve her favorite teacher ("Mars vs. Mars") or a Russian immigrant seeking her lost love ("Ruskie Business"). But here's the catch: We arrive at this conclusion about the general reliability of inference to the best explanation through ... *an inference to the best explanation*! After all, we don't need to chalk up the past success of inference to the best explanation to its basic trustworthiness. It could be that Veronica and everyone else who relies on that form of inference has just gotten lucky. But we reject that explanation as lacking, among other things, consilience and simplicity, which makes it a much worse explanation of the track record of success of inference to the best explanation than its simply being a good guide to truth would be. But explaining the success of inference to the best explanation by calling it a good guide to truth is circular. It would be like trying to determine if Weevil is a liar by asking him if he lies, all the while assuming that he probably wouldn't lie about that sort of thing.

Or perhaps we believe that inference to the best explanation is likely to serve us well in the future simply because it's served us so well in the past. But that just leads us into a deeper problem, one associated with the great Scottish philosopher David Hume (1711–1776).[4] Hume asked why we typically think that the future will be (more or less) like the present and the past. It seems possible in principle for things to change very suddenly— one moment you're a happy popular girl dating the most eligible bachelor in Neptune, the next moment you're a lonely social pariah with a dead best friend. One very tempting answer is that, while things can sometimes change very suddenly, we know from experience that they usually don't. The problem with that answer is that all of our experience of things not suddenly changing is of the past and the present; we've never experienced the future. So in order to conclude that the future will be like the past and the present, we appeal to the fact that things generally haven't changed too suddenly in the past and assume that this trend will continue into the future. But that's just another case of circular reasoning.

Me and Inference to the Best Explanation Used to Be Friends (a Long Time Ago)

If we have no good reason to trust inferences to the best explanation, maybe we should just avoid them. We certainly haven't been given any reason to think that they are a good guide to truth. And if all that jury foreperson Veronica has to go on is an unjustified method of inference, something akin to testimony from an unreliable witness, maybe the right move would have been to acquit those 09-ers all along. After all, if we don't know whose story to believe, isn't the right verdict an acquittal?

The rub is that Veronica can't help but to use inference to the best explanation. None of us can. And that's what makes this topic such an interesting philosophical puzzle. Pausing to examine how we acquire most of our beliefs, we see that we use inference to the best explanation *all the time*.

Let's return to when Veronica looks at that Little League picture and suddenly realizes that Beaver is a killer. Maybe she's being a bit hasty. Maybe she should refrain from assigning a cause to the crash when she didn't really see Beaver rig the explosives. But, following that logic, *she shouldn't even be sure there was a crash*, since she didn't see that either. Veronica came across a cliff face, a fallen bus, and a bunch of 09-ers claiming that they had seen the bus go over. The best explanation for all those data is that there really was a bus crash; but Veronica wouldn't be entitled to that conclusion if she couldn't use inference to the best explanation.

Try to imagine what the world would be like if you could act only on what you saw and what definitely followed from what you saw. Weevil didn't see Felix Toombs murdered, but Weevil would hardly have been able to function if he had tried to live as though that murder never happened. We actually see something like this when Logan, who didn't see his mother die, refuses to believe that she is dead: he's unable to move on with his life as a result.

It gets still worse. So far, I have assumed that Veronica at least has reason to believe what she sees, even if she can't make any inferences beyond that. But what does she really see? Even if she had been present at the bus crash, she would have been directly aware only of something that looked like a bus going over something that looked like a cliff. And that's the sort of thing that can be faked. In fact, it was Curly Moran's ability to fake bus crashes that led Beaver to recruit him as an unwitting accomplice in the first place. It's natural to infer that a bus actually did go over a cliff, but there are infinitely many other possible explanations that we would have to consider if we couldn't rely on inference to the best explanation.

The philosopher René Descartes (1596–1650), for instance, famously argued that, for all he knew, there could be an evil demon planting illusions directly into his mind.[5] Or we could all be like Duncan, suffering from hallucinations because we've decided to forego our psych meds for a few days. Either hypothesis would explain our sensory input. Those explanations may not be as good as the assumption that our senses reliably reflect an external world, but why should that matter if we've tossed aside inference to the best explanation?[6]

Kickstarting Inductive Inference

The legitimacy of inference to the best explanation is a philosophical puzzle. I don't have a clever answer here and, as far as I know, no one does. The best that anyone has done is to give us reason to think that maybe we were asking the wrong question all along.

Let's return for a moment to deductive inferences, where the truth of what you infer is guaranteed by the truth of the beliefs it's based on. You can't get more certainty than that. But suppose someone doesn't trust logic and denies that deductive inferences are any good. Imagine, for instance, Sean arguing that while, yes, one of the people in the room stole the money and, yes, no one other than him could have stolen the money, he still wasn't the one who stole the money. And let's pretend that Sean isn't just grasping at straws, but that he genuinely doesn't see why he should make what the rest of us would say is a perfectly good deductive inference. What could we say to him?

It turns out that what we can say in defense of deductive inferences is about the same as what we can say in defense of inference to the best explanation—pretty much nothing. If Sean has these strange views about logic and refuses to acknowledge the validity of basic deductive inferences, we can't even prove to him that he's being inconsistent. Whatever facts we cite to defend our way of making inferences, they won't lead to any conclusion unless we make an inference on the basis of them. But if someone doubts the validity of the very rules that allow us to make inferences, we're completely hamstrung.[7] The philosopher Nelson Goodman (1906–1998) took this as evidence that we somehow must be asking the wrong question when we ask what justifies our inferences.[8] The question is no good because there simply isn't anything that would count as a good answer.

What we should be looking for, Goodman argues, is not a *justification* of our patterns of reasoning, but a consistent *description* of them. Forget what sorts of explanations we *should* favor; the best we can hope for is a theory of which ones we actually *do* favor. We can also strive for consistency; for, even if we can't justify our inferences from the outside, we can at least hope that they hang together well internally.

We could say something similar about Veronica's inferences to the best explanation. On the one hand, there doesn't seem to be anything that justifies her basic pattern of reasoning. On the other hand, what could *possibly* justify it? We should be looking instead for whether she uses the same process and rules consistently. She seems to be doing well on this count, since, as we've seen, she uses the same methods in the juryroom that she employs when hunting a bus crasher.

There is something admittedly unsatisfying about this answer. If Veronica is going to drive Beaver to suicide, it would be nice if she could do so on the basis of beliefs that were justified by some fully justified procedure. But that might not be in the cards. Everyone has to start somewhere, and maybe inference to the best explanation is just where Veronica needs to start. What makes her a good reasoner is that she generally uses a consistent set of intuitively plausible criteria to evaluate explanations and to make inferences. In the end, that might be the best any of us can do. That—and occasionally outsmarting the FBI to smuggle a baby to Mexico ("Donut Run").

Notes

1. Peter Lipton, *Inference to the Best Explanation* (New York: Routledge, 2004).

2. Many of the terms for these positive features come from the work of contemporary philosopher Paul R. Thagard. See his "The Best Explanation: Criteria for Theory Choice," *The Journal of Philosophy*, 75 (1978): 76–92.

3. For more on the principle that simpler explanations are better, see Chapter 14 in this volume," by Andrew Zimmerman Jones.

4. David Hume, *An Enquiry Concerning Human Understanding: A critical edition*, vol. 3 (New York: Oxford University Press, 2000), 108–118.

5. René Descartes, *Meditations on First Philosophy*, trans. Donald A. Cress (Indianapolis, IN: Hackett, 1993), 13–16.

6. The point about doubting sensory perception is controversial. Some philosophers think that what we're aware of more than just something bus-looking going over something cliff-looking— namely that we're somehow directly aware of the bus going over the cliff. But, even if we accept this account of things we immediately see, an awful lot of knowledge is still left unjustified.

7. This point about inferences being deniable was brought home to the philosophical community in a short whimsical article by Lewis Carroll. See Lewis Carroll, "What the Tortoise Said to Achilles," *Mind*, 4 (1895): 278–280.

8. Nelson Goodman, *Fact, Fiction, and Forecast* (New York: Bobbs-Merrill Company, 1965), 62–64.

Part VI

VERONICA MARS IS A MARSHMALLOW

INVESTIGATING VERONICA'S QUEST FOR IDENTITY

16

Veronica Mars—She's a Marshmallow

James B. South

The first season of *Veronica Mars* is best understood as the portrayal of a young woman's attempt to forge a new identity. This might not be the most obvious of claims. After all, what we see most in the series is a witty, self-assured, and knowing young woman who's a student by day and a detective most of the rest of her time. The viewer could be excused for thinking that Veronica already has an identity. In one sense, that's true. The character of Veronica is clearly drawn in the series and, as viewers, we know both her strengths and her weaknesses. Yet there is a sense in which Veronica doesn't really have an identity at the start of the season. Even though Veronica realizes that she's changed from who she was only a year before, it's unclear whom she thinks she's changed into. Becoming a different girl will be her challenge over the course of the first season. In talking about her forging an identity, then, I'm talking about a different feature of the character portrayed in the series. The meaning of my claim and the evidence for it will emerge by looking in detail at some scenes from the first season.

In addition, I want to explore the significance of the fact that Veronica Mars has photography as a hobby. Of course, photography is not shown as a hobby at all in the show, but rather

Veronica Mars and Philosophy: Investigating the Mysteries of Life (Which is a Bitch Until You Die), First Edition. Edited by George A. Dunn.
© 2014 John Wiley & Sons, Inc. Published 2014 by Wiley Blackwell.

as an instrument used in her work as a detective. Nonetheless, I think it is important to take seriously Veronica's claim that photography is her hobby. It's not just that she uses the camera in her detective work, but that her way of situating herself in her world is indebted to—or analogous to—the work of a camera.

"No Longer That Girl"

In the first episode of the first season we get a glimpse of Veronica's relation to her humanity when her teacher Mrs. Murphy asks her to read and comment on a passage from Alexander Pope's (1688–1744) *An Essay on Man*.

VERONICA	Hope springs eternal in the human breast:
	Man never is, but always to be blest.
	The soul, uneasy and confined from home,
	Rests and expatiates in a life to come.
MRS. MURPHY	And what do you suppose Pope meant by that?
VERONICA	Life's a bitch until you die.

There's predictable laughter from the other students at this answer. Mrs. Murphy continues, "Okay, thank you, Ms. Mars, for that succinct and somewhat inappropriate response." The teacher proceeds to explain that what Pope really means is "that the thing that keeps us powering through life's defeats is our faith in a better life yet to come." This scene, which nicely sets up Veronica's self-image as hardened and cynical, is instructive because it strikingly creates a contrast that can be misleading. The two extremes—"Life's a bitch until you die" and "faith in a better life to come"—don't exhaust the ways of understanding one's place in the world.

Veronica is initially justified in finding the lesson drawn by the teacher less than compelling. She has found her life irrevocably altered in multiple ways. Her best friend, Lilly Kane, was murdered, her father lost his job as sheriff as the result of an apparently bungled investigation into Lilly's death, and Veronica lost her social status and former friends. Subsequently her mother, Lianne Mars, left home, apparently unable to deal with the stress of it all. In addition to all this misfortune, Veronica, trying to show her former friends that she was unaffected by "their whispers and backstabbing," had attended a party at which she was drugged and then raped. As she puts it during a voiceover explaining why she never told her father about her rape, "I never told my dad. I'm not sure what he would have done with that information but no good would have come of it. And what does it matter? I'm no longer that girl" ("Pilot").

She's Pretty *Noir*

Even though Veronica realizes that she's changed, it's unclear whom she thinks she has changed into. As we discover quite quickly, there is another sense, too—this one quite literal—in which it is true to say that Veronica does not know who she is. In the episode "Like a Virgin," Abel Koontz reveals that Jake Kane, Lilly's father, may in fact be Veronica's father. Veronica lives with that possibility until the final episode of the season, when it's finally revealed who her real father is.

With all these misfortunes, identity crises, and the horror of her rape, Veronica appears to have quite understandably taken a cynical stance toward the world and others, which she often expresses with a very dry wit. This wit and cynicism is evident in the opening voiceover of the extended version of the first episode (available on DVD) as Veronica sits in front of a sleazy motel, ironically named the Camelot, waiting to take a picture of someone cheating.

> Forty dollars an hour is cheap compared to the long-term financial security sordid photography can secure for you, your offspring, your next lover. But do us a favor. If it's you in there,

dispense with the cuddling. This motel tryst? It is what it is. Make it quick. That person sitting in a car across the street might have a Calculus exam in five … make that four hours and she can't leave until she gets the money shot.

The attitude on display in this voiceover reveals the series' roots in *film noir*.[1] Compare this voiceover with the classic assessment of the detective in Raymond Chandler's (1888–1959) essay "The Simple Art of Murder":

> Down these mean streets a man must go who is not himself mean, who is neither tarnished nor afraid. The detective must be a complete man and a common man and yet an unusual man. He must be, to use a rather weathered phrase, a man of honor. He talks as the man of his age talks, that is, with rude wit, a lively sense of the grotesque, a disgust for sham, and a contempt for pettiness.[2]

With the exception of the masculine inflection, the attributes of a detective described by Chandler are given ample acknowledgment throughout the first season as Veronica repeatedly takes on petty and corrupt people who are out to harm others. Throughout the season Veronica exhibits "rude wit, a lively sense of the grotesque, a disgust for sham, and a contempt for pettiness." In the first episode alone, she takes on both school officials and the sheriff, outwitting both easily. But these connections with the *noir* tradition don't tell the full story of the season. Indeed they might blind us to how different Veronica is from the typical *noir* detective.

Steven Sanders provides a compelling précis of the philosophical commitments of *noir*:

> Above all, film noir depicts a world of characters trapped in circumstances that they did not wholly create and from which they cannot break free, characters helplessly isolated and all but immobilized in moral dilemmas whose implications they must follow out, as it were, to the end of the night.[3]

It is certainly the case that Veronica begins the season trapped in a set of circumstances that she didn't create. Her voiceover in the pilot is all *noir* jadedness, and it concludes with the lesson she's learned from her work "in this business" of doing surveillance and private investigation: "the people you love let you down." That sounds as cynical and realistic as the bleakest *noir*. And by the end of the episode she's found this attitude reinforced, as she discovers that her father, Keith Mars, hasn't been truthful to her about her mother's departure. What would it mean for her to break free of those circumstances in which she finds herself and to learn something different from the cynical lessons she's internalized from her experience in "this business"?

She's Mushy

Getting to the truth of her mother's departure will be part of Veronica's work throughout season 1. As she states in the voiceover that concludes the pilot,

> I used to think I knew what tore our family apart. Now I'm sure I don't. But I promise this. I will find out what really happened and I will bring this family back together again. I'm sorry, is that mushy? Well, you know what they say. Veronica Mars, she's a marshmallow.

Now, describing herself as a marshmallow is clearly meant ironically. In the course of the episode we've seen her get the better of the sheriff, a gang of petty criminals, and her school's principal. She's no marshmallow in that respect. There's some truth to her claim, though. Mushy hope serves an important function on her way to becoming the self she is at the end of the first season. There's a clear symbol of Veronica's mushiness in the pilot: a unicorn music box on her desk at Mars Investigations, which her mother left as a gift when she departed. We see Veronica staring at this music box and thinking about her mother as it plays the Beatles song "All You Need is Love."

Standing behind all her acts of detection in the first season is Veronica's search for answers to three significant questions: (1) Who raped her? (2) Who killed Lilly Kane? and (3) How can she put her family back together? In the course of dealing with the second and third questions—the first remains unsolved in the first season—Veronica comes up against the limits of her interpretation of Pope, and her *noir* attitude is shown to be inadequate. The even more important question standing behind all of these questions is this: Who is Veronica Mars, if she is no longer "that girl"?

Veronica's Voiceovers

Let's consider a scene from "Credit Where Credit's Due." Veronica is sent to "newspaper class" by the guidance counselor, who's called her "disconnected and passionless." "Maybe I could just take pictures," Veronica suggests to her teacher, Mallory Dent, explaining that she has some experience with a camera. When Ms. Dent begins, condescendingly, to explain how to work a 35-millimeter camera, Veronica pulls her own camera out of her bag and begins describing some of its features in a way that displays her superior knowledge of cameras. Taking this demonstration with good humor, Ms. Dent provides Veronica with her first story to cover.

This scene is worth pausing over, because it explicitly links Veronica's "disconnected" emotional state to her desire to take pictures. Indeed, throughout the first season, her camera and questions about photographs are central to Veronica's activities and to the mysteries she's trying to solve. And, as we shall see, her use of a camera, as well as her obsession with various photographs, is related to her disconnectedness and lack of passion. Moreover, this relation between her disconnectedness and photography is a quite specific one: it's an image of a certain sort of skeptical position she takes towards the world and herself.

In his book *The World Viewed: Reflections on the Ontology of Film*, the philosopher Stanley Cavell provides an account of the relation between photography and subjectivity:

> So far as photography satisfied a wish, it satisfied … the human wish, intensifying in the West since the Reformation, to escape subjectivity and metaphysical isolation—a wish for the power to reach this world, having for so long tried, at last hopelessly, to manifest fidelity to another.[4]

Veronica's constant voiceovers are a classic tool for representing the distance between self and world. In their "objectivity"—the way they describe in apparently authoritative ways the actions, beliefs, and emotions of the participants, including Veronica—they suggest a kind of knowledge about others and the world that may be more wished for than real. And indeed, one way to mark the rise of the Cavellian notion of subjectivity is to yoke it to the rise of the need for conviction in knowledge, that is, to a kind of certainty. The rapid dissolution of Veronica's pre-catastrophe world would be devastating for anyone. It's not surprising, then, that she retreats to a standpoint of false certainty. Just as it makes sense to see Veronica as no longer "that girl," it makes sense that she would grasp at any position in the world that allowed her to survive, to rebuild a self, regardless of the grounds for that rebuilding.

At the beginning of the series Veronica has rebuilt her "self," albeit as one with a heightened sense of subjectivity, which makes her role as detective and outside observer of humanity explicable. Her outsider status is brought home again and again throughout the season, perhaps nowhere more forcefully than in the first episode, where Veronica sits by herself at a high school lunch table, looking at her former friends. She provides the following voiceover:

> I used to sit there. At that table. It's not like my family met the minimum net worth requirement. My dad didn't own his own airline like John Enbom's or serve as ambassador to Belgium like Shelly Pomeroy's, but my dad used to be the sheriff and that had a certain cachet. Let's be honest, though. The only reason I was allowed past the velvet ropes was Duncan Kane. Son of software billionaire, Jake Kane, he used to be my boyfriend. Then one day, with no warning, he ended things. And let's not forget Logan Echolls. His dad makes twenty million a picture. You probably own his action figure. Every school has an obligatory psychotic jackass. He's ours. ("Pilot")

At this point Wallace sits down at the table with Veronica, remarking that she looks "hypnotized." The term is telling. Veronica is surveying, as if looking from a distance, her old life. She might as well be looking at a photo of her former friends.

Veronica's Photography

How are photography and subjectivity related? Of our modern experience of subjectivity, Cavell writes: "At some point the unhinging of our consciousness from the world interposed our subjectivity between us and our presentness to our world."[5] Photography provides us with a means to escape our subjectivity and to reach the world. As Cavell explains:

> Photography maintains the presentness of the world by accepting our absence from it. The reality in a photograph is present to me while I am not present to it; and a world I know, and see, but to which I am nevertheless not present (through no fault of my subjectivity), is a world past.[6]

Why am I not present, while the reality in a photograph is present? "Photography overcomes subjectivity ... by automatism, by removing the human agent from the task of reproduction."[7] What's crucial is the way this automatism relieves us of the work of being present in the world. Cavell concludes:

> Our condition has become one in which our natural mode of perception is to view, feeling unseen. We do not so much look at the world as look *out at* it, from behind the self. It is our fantasies, now all but completely thwarted and out of hand, which are unseen and must be kept unseen. As if we could no longer hope that anyone might share them ... So we are less than ever in a position to marry them to the world.[8]

The image of our isolated subjectivity that Cavell provides in this passage—"looking out at the world from behind the self"— is also an apt image for the relation of the photographer, her camera, and the world. Accordingly, when Veronica takes pictures of the world, those pictures don't include her and usually don't have an effect on her, except perhaps to make her lose sleep before a Calculus exam.

Cavell suggests that one feature of photography that we find attractive is the way in which the automatism of the photograph—like the photograph-like depiction provided by a voiceover—makes it seem that we're not responsible for our isolation, that our isolation is natural. In this way the photograph provides us with a connection to the world, but at the price of our giving up on finding ourselves. Of course, such isolation isn't natural. But if we've retreated from the task of connecting with the world, photographs give us the only reality we can know. Photographs in this sense relieve us from responsibility. But photographs also might cause us "to be wakened, so that we may stop withdrawing our longings further inside ourselves," since they "convince us of the world's reality."[9]

Putting these ideas together yields a way to interpret Veronica's status at the beginning of the series. We know that her reconstructed self, supplanting "that girl," is one that is isolated from the world. She uses photography as a means to relieve herself from the pain of her isolation, as a means to connect with reality without bearing any responsibility for it. The series augments our awareness of Veronica's isolation by using the device of voiceover narrative. The heightened sense of objectivity and isolation present in her ubiquitous voiceovers reinforces the way in which she interposes her "self" between her "true being" and the world. Thus Veronica is doubly at a distance from reality: she views the world as from behind her self, and she describes it in knowing, cynical terms, assuming an objectivity that's only possible on the basis of her isolation. But what's the status of the self that Veronica has reconstructed?

We can't simply assume that there's a true self and a world and that all we need to do is figure out a way to connect them. That would be to ignore, as Cavell puts it, "the fact that the world is *already* drawn by fantasy."[10] Presumably the world is so drawn in many ways by social, cultural, and political fantasies. Indeed, these are all elements of fantasy that get addressed in the series. For example, the perpetual class conflict between the 09-ers and the remaining students, including Veronica, is clearly represented. As we've seen, part of Veronica's sense of being an outsider is dependent on her being cast out of the group once her social status is diminished. So, too, the second season of the series portrays quite clearly the effect of politics and its attendant fantasies on everyone's lives. These elements of fantasy, as important as they are, can't be addressed here. Instead let's focus on the cultural fantasy of the happy family, since it's the one to which Veronica is most committed and the one that, through most of the season, thwarts her attempts to find a desire or a longing that can be married to the world.

"All You Need Is Love"

The first episode shows us how important reuniting her family is to Veronica. As we have already noted, in the closing scene of the episode she vows, with self-reported mushiness, to reunite her family. Earlier in the episode she tells us that, a month after her father lost his position as sheriff, her mother left town, leaving behind only a unicorn music box and a note saying that she would come back for Veronica. Veronica's decision to hold on to the music box, despite her determination to take on a new self-image as a spectator, shows that she still clings to the past and to her childhood fantasy of what family life should be like. The sentimentality of the kitschy unicorn music box, as well as the treacly version of the song it plays, remind us of just how mushy Veronica is underneath her hard exterior.[11] Perhaps she could accept her teacher's interpretation of Pope's poem: faith in a better life to come.

In the first episode Celeste Kane drops by Mars Investigations, to hire Keith to find out whether Jake is having an affair. While staking out the Camelot Hotel on that assignment, Veronica takes a photograph that leads her to the discovery that her mother is back in town and apparently somehow involved with Jake. But when she asks her father about the license plate, he abruptly announces that he's decided not to take the case. He later tells her that he ran the plate, which only confirmed his suspicion that Jake Kane was involved in some sort of corporate espionage. "It's dangerous," he says. "We don't get paid enough." Veronica knows that Keith is lying to her, but she doesn't know why. Her response isn't to question Keith further, but to fall back on her new persona as detective and to try to find out the truth about her mother. She believes that, if she solves that mystery, her mother will return to the family.

In the course of Veronica's investigations, Able Koontz reveals to her that her mother and Jake Kane were high school sweethearts and that it's possible that Veronica is Jake's daughter, which would mean that Duncan, whom she had been dating until shortly before Lilly's death, would be her half-brother ("Like a Virgin"). Later in the season Duncan runs away from Neptune, when he becomes aware that Veronica regards him as suspect in Lilly's death ("Weapons of Class Destruction"). Veronica agrees to help the Kanes find Duncan, on condition that they drop charges against Eli "Weevil" Navarro, who had broken into their house looking for clues to Lilly's murder ("Hot Dogs"). Keith eventually finds Duncan and returns him to his parents, expecting to receive the $50,000 reward they had promised for Duncan's return. Celeste points out, though, that Veronica had made a different deal ("A Trip to the Dentist"). But, when pressed, the Kanes agree to pay Keith the $50,000, but only on condition that Veronica renounce any future claims on the Kane estate. Since Veronica might be Jake's daughter, Keith realizes that she could potentially be signing away millions of dollars if she accepts the deal. Veronica looks at the contract Keith sets before her, glances briefly at Keith, and then signs the document. She then looks again at Keith, who shows her the results of the paternity test that demonstrate that he's her real father ("Leave It to Beaver").

As for her mother, as the season wears on, Veronica discovers that Lianne is an alcoholic. Cashing in her college savings, Veronica funds her mother's trip to rehab ("Betty and Veronica"). But Lianne leaves rehab early and returns to drinking, which Veronica finds out when she sips from the bottle of "water" her mother had been drinking, only to discover it contained alcohol ("Leave It to Beaver"). When Veronica confronts her mother, all she can say for herself is: "Veronica, it's not easy." "I know it's not," Veronica replies. "I bet on you, and I lost. I've been doing that my whole life. And I'm through" ("Leave It to Beaver").

There are multiple ways to interpret that final "I know it's not." One would be to see it as a simple acknowledgment that her mother can't stop drinking. More interesting, though, is another meaning the line can bear, namely that Veronica has learned that giving up certain fantasies is necessary, albeit painful. The fantasies that Veronica renounces revolve around her "mushy" view of family life. In giving them up, she begins to achieve a new self. We see this clearly in her conviction—based on her heart rather than on scientific evidence—that Keith is her father or, to put it another way, that she doesn't want to be a Kane. She has made herself Keith's daughter in a way that runs deeper than blood. As Lianne shows, blood isn't enough.

"I Was Hoping It Would Be You"

Despite the many *noir* elements and despite Veronica's harrowing adventures, we find at the end of the first season that the center of the show is the relationship between Veronica and her father. It's her father's constant support—even when there is skepticism about his status as father—that helps Veronica achieve a new self-awareness, one that allows her to acknowledge Keith as her father, as someone who won't let her down. At the end of the season she has broken through to a new self-understanding, as illustrated by the final scene. She hears a knock on the door, opens it, and smiles. We viewers don't see who's at the door. Veronica simply says, "I was hoping it would be you." Of course, it turns out to be Logan, whose relationship with Veronica will prompt her to grow and define herself in the seasons to come.

Acknowledgment

I want to thank George Dunn for his patience and dedication to this volume. In addition, I am happy to thank both him and William Irwin for very helpful comments on a draft of this chapter. Finally, an even earlier draft was read by my colleague Susanne Foster, who made helpful comments on that version.

Notes

1. The *noir* elements in the series have been emphasized by others who wrote on the series; indeed the creator of the show edited a volume of essays on the show entitled *Neptune Noir*. See especially Amanda Ann Klein, "The Noir of Neptune," in Rob Thomas, ed., *Neptune Noir* (Dallas, TX: BenBella Books, 2007), 82–92. For more on the conventions of *noir* fiction, see Chapter 5 in this volume, by Daniel Wack.
2. Raymond Chandler, "The Simple Art of Murder," in Frank MacShane, ed., *Raymond Chandler: Later Novels and Other Writings* (New York: Library of America, 1995), 992.
3. Steven M. Sanders, "Film Noir and the Meaning of Life," in Mark T. Conard, ed., *The Philosophy of Film Noir* (Lexington: University Press of Kentucky, 2007), 93.
4. Stanley Cavell, *The World Viewed: Reflections on the Ontology of Film* (Cambridge, MA: Harvard University Press, 1979), 21. For more on Cavell, see, again, Chapter 5 in this volume, by Daniel Wack.
5. Cavell, *The World Viewed*, 22.
6. Ibid., 23.
7. Ibid.
8. Ibid., 102
9. Ibid.
10. Ibid.
11. In a series as self-consciously aware of popular culture as *Veronica Mars*, I cannot help but connect up this unicorn music box with the film *Blade Runner*, in which an origami unicorn is used to suggest, on one plausible reading, that the protagonist of the movie is not actually a human. There is a sense in which Veronica has renounced her humanity by failing to marry her fantasies to the world.

Notes on Contributors
Under Investigation

Kasey Butcher is currently working on her PhD at Miami University, where she studies twentieth-century multi-ethnic literature and teaches first-year composition courses. She also researches and writes about feminism and girlhood, trying to harness some pixie spy magic.

Dereck Coatney received his MA in philosophy from Indiana University in Indianapolis and is currently a philosophy graduate student in Tulane University's doctoral program, where he's preparing to write his dissertation on Friedrich Nietzsche. Dereck was also a contributor to *The Hunger Games and Philosophy*. Like Veronica, he finds the lure of seeking the truth irresistible, not despite but because of its possible dangers.

George A. Dunn is editor of the forthcoming *Avatar and Philosophy*, co-editor of *True Blood and Philosophy*, *The Hunger Games and Philosophy*, and *Sons of Anarchy and Philosophy* and contributor to numerous other books on pop culture topics such as *Iron Man*, *Mad Men*, *Terminator*, and *Battlestar Galactica*. He lectures on philosophy and religion at

Veronica Mars and Philosophy: Investigating the Mysteries of Life (Which is a Bitch Until You Die), First Edition. Edited by George A. Dunn.
© 2014 John Wiley & Sons, Inc. Published 2014 by Wiley Blackwell.

the University of Indianapolis and at the Ningbo Institute of Technology in Zhejiang, China, where his students affectionately describe him as the "obligatory psychotic jackass."

Paul Hammond is a long-time *Veronica Mars* fan and a first-time contributor to Wiley's Philosophy and Pop Culture series. His philosophical interests include social and political thought and twentieth-century French philosophy, especially the work of Gilles Deleuze. He's also a PhD student and an instructor in philosophy at the University of Memphis, where he divides his time between teaching, researching, and picking up the odd shift at his local Java the Hut.

William Irwin is chair and professor of philosophy at King's College, Pennsylvania. In addition to publishing in leading philosophy journals, he is the general editor of the Blackwell Philosophy and Pop Culture series and the volume editor of *Metallica and Philosophy* and *Black Sabbath and Philosophy*. Like Keith Mars, Irwin used to drive a '77 Trans-Am, Blue Oyster Cult in the 8-track, foxy, stacked blond riding shotgun, racing for pink slips. Wait a minute! He was never that cool. Then again, neither was Keith Mars.

Andrew Zimmerman Jones is the About.com physics guide and co-author of *String Theory for Dummies*. He has contributed to a variety of publications, including the PBS NOVA Physics blog, and to books on *The Hunger Games*, *The Avengers*, *The Big Bang Theory*, *Green Lantern*, *Ender's Game*, and other pop culture topics. Andrew spends the rest of his time with his wife and two sons, using Keith Mars as his parenting role model and looking forward to the day when he can teach them how to use a stun gun.

Catlyn Origitano is a PhD candidate in philosophy at Marquette University. Her main area of research is ethics, specifically the role of imagination in our everyday moral understanding and deliberation. When not teaching, Catlyn can be found training cartoon birds to braid her hair.

Jordan Pascoe teaches at Manhattan College in New York City, where she writes about Kant, feminist philosophy, and African philosophy. She lives in Brooklyn with her husband and two awesome stepkids. She admits that under her angry young woman shell there's a slightly less angry young woman who is just dying to bake you something. She has never taken a purity test.

Megan M. Peters is a PhD candidate at Miami University in Oxford, Ohio, where she teaches composition, business writing, American literature, and women's studies. She is currently writing a dissertation on the intersection of gender and nation in metafiction from the 1960s and 1970s. She's always trying to find the best way to annoy her students—"annoy like the wind!"

Jon Robson teaches at the University of Nottingham in the UK. He mainly works in aesthetics, ethics, metaphysics, and the philosophy of religion. He especially enjoys combining these different areas in weird and (hopefully) wonderful ways. Above all, though—and this is important, you remember this—he used to be cool.

James Rocha is an assistant professor of philosophy and of women and gender studies at Louisiana State University, where he specializes in applied ethics, Kant's moral and political philosophy, philosophy of sex, and philosophy and popular culture. His philosophy and popular culture contributions include works on *Psych*, *Curb Your Enthusiasm*, *The Wire*, and *Dungeons & Dragons*. His students consider his grading to be persnickety, but in his off hours he can be even persnicketier.

Mona Rocha is an instructor in women and gender studies and history at Louisiana State University, where she is finishing her dissertation on the women of the Weather Underground Organization. Her contributions to philosophy and pop culture include essays on *Psych*, *The Wire*, and *Dungeons & Dragons*. She loves to discuss gender norms and relationships with her students and will tell anyone waiting for a macchiato that Veronica is way too good for Logan.

Rejena Saulsberry is an assistant professor of criminal justice at the University of Arkansas at Monticello, where she lectures on the intersection of law, race, gender, and popular culture. She does not now, nor will she ever, own a hacky sack.

James B. South is associate professor and associate dean for faculty in the College of Arts and Sciences at Marquette University. He is the editor of the journal *Philosophy and Theology*. He edited *Buffy the Vampire Slayer and Philosophy* and co-edited *James Bond and Philosophy*, *Buffy Goes Dark*, and *Mad Men and Philosophy*. In addition, he's written essays on movies, comic books, and popular music. He has also published extensively in late medieval and Renaissance philosophy, where he focuses on fifteenth- and sixteenth-century Aristotelianism. He often wonders which Gilmore Girl Veronica would think he is.

Daniel Wack is assistant professor of philosophy at Knox College. He works primarily on philosophy of film and action theory. He would especially like to thank Erica Holberg for watching and talking about *Veronica Mars* with him. Like Veronica, he has always taken Encyclopedia Brown as a role model.

Daniel A. Wilkenfeld is a senior lecturer at Ohio State University, where he specializes in philosophy of science and epistemology. Most of his classes respond well to the voice mail inspirational quote of the day.

Index